D1457363

GOAL SETTING

a motivational technique that works!

EDWIN A. LOCKE
University of Maryland

GARY P. LATHAM
University of Washington

PRENTICE-HALL, INC., *Englewood Cliffs, NJ* 07632

Library of Congress Cataloging in Publication Data

LOCKE, EDWIN A.
  Goal setting.

  Includes bibliographical references and index.
  1. Goal setting in personnel management.   2. Employee
motivation.   I. Latham, Gary P.   II. Title.
HF5549.5.G6L62   1984   658.3′142   83-9510
ISBN   0-13-357467-9

To
ANNE and JOANNA
and
SHERRY, BRYAN, and BRANDON

Editorial/production supervision and interior design: Maureen Wilson
Cover design: Ray Lundgren
Manufacturing buyer: Ed O'Dougherty

This book is available to businesses and organizations at
a special discount when ordered in large quantities.
For information, contact
Prentice-Hall, Inc., General Book Marketing,
Special Sales Division, Englewood Cliffs, NJ   07632.

Printed in the United States of America
10   9   8   7   6

ISBN 0-13-357467-9

PRENTICE-HALL INTERNATIONAL, INC., *London*
PRENTICE-HALL OF AUSTRALIA PTY. LIMITED, *Sydney*
EDITORA PRENTICE-HALL DO BRASIL, LTDA., *Rio de Janeiro*
PRENTICE-HALL CANADA INC., *Toronto*
PRENTICE-HALL OF INDIA PRIVATE LIMITED, *New Delhi*
PRENTICE-HALL OF JAPAN, INC., *Tokyo*
PRENTICE-HALL OF SOUTHEAST ASIA PTE. LTD., *Singapore*
WHITEHALL BOOKS LIMITED, *Wellington, New Zealand*

Contents

Foreword

As long as there are two managers left in the world, they will spend their time discussing business with each other. And just as surely as they discuss business, they will argue about how to improve each other's productivity. For employee productivity is the very heart and soul of this shifting and subtle activity we call management.

All managers want to lift their associates' performance to higher levels of efficiency and quality. Changing business and technology and quickening international competition testify that doing the same old things a little faster will no longer suffice. To remain competitive we must also do things better and more creatively than we have in the past.

A company's investment in human capital—its employees—is its primary opportunity for improvement. Not surprisingly, modern management has become enamored with a number of fashionable new techniques from "Theory Z" to "Quality Circles," all of which promise to help raise employee productivity. But while the search for lasting employee motivation is certainly laudable, too often it becomes little more than a series of flirtations with seductive-sounding systems.

Thus, when Edwin Locke and Gary Latham present their comprehensive book, *Goal Setting: A Motivational Technique That Works!*, it would be no real surprise if the prospective reader, jaded by exposure to other modish techniques, had a somewhat subdued initial reaction. After all, isn't "goal setting" a seemingly self-evident concept? And don't all American managers practice that technique now anyway?

Not necessarily, argue Locke and Latham. In fact, few managers today set meaningful goals and this hinders productivity and job satisfaction among their employees. Perhaps the self-evident nature of the concept causes many business people to overlook it.

Some American managers find it subliminally unsettling to set performance goals for others. As schoolchildren many of us were taught the values of self-reliance and encouraged to hitch our wagons to a star. Striving to meet personal goals has been a recurring theme for American entrepreneurs, folk heroes, and sports stars. But we have never been particularly comfortable in setting goals for others. There is something in our national psyche that views goal setting for subordinates and colleagues as vaguely dictatorial and stifling to their own sense of initiative and direction.

To the great credit of Locke and Latham, their book shows that performance goals, far from being limiting and dictatorial, can be fulfilling and liberating experiences for individual employees, entire departments, and the company as a whole. Goals provide direction for efforts and guard against dissipating energy through lack of understanding of what is expected. Feedback regarding progress in relation to goals tracks employee improvement, relays that improvement to the employee, and thus builds self-confidence. Surpassing goals may provide the only challenge in an inherently unexciting activity.

Most importantly, goal setting is a powerful message to the organization, emphasizing to each employee that his or her superiors not only are aware of this individual's presence, but also that they have such specific knowledge of his or her potential contribution that they can factor it into their plans for the entire concern. When goals are set for the individual, for the department, and for the organization, the employee is freed from having to wonder what, if anything, is expected of him or her and can direct more energy to meeting the challenge.

The authors spend considerable time exploring how to make goal setting part and parcel of the manager's "art." In very practical terms they discuss how to set goals and what sort of goals to set. They include suggestions on obtaining commitment for goals, implementing them, and assessing feedback. The authors also point out the traps and dangers in goal setting, along with comments on special situations, such as goal setting for organized labor and strategic goal setting by senior management.

That the book will be valuable to skeptics as well as to those already sympathetic to goal setting is attributable to the authors' scrupulous inclusion of documentation. Though their own enthusiasm for goal setting is obvious, they never take it for granted that their readers come predisposed to share their opinion; consequently, Locke and Latham cite numerous studies and cases to support their conclusions. By thus subjecting their concepts to critical scrutiny, the authors are able to take goal setting out of the realm of untested cliches and give it power as a concept in its own right.

In the process we become aware that goal setting is much more than the latest management fad. It is an essential management skill inherent in all the other popular motivational techniques. It is as fundamental to all management styles as reading music is to the playing of all instruments. It is not just a technique that succeeds, it is the very reason why other techniques are able to succeed.

S. Bruce Smart, Jr.

Chairman and Chief Executive Officer
Continental Group

Preface

The world economy is faced with a crisis unprecedented since the great depression. Plagued by high inflation, massive unemployment, high interest rates, an increasing number of business failures, and huge government deficits, most countries, including the United States, are desperately looking for solutions. The need for solutions is made all the more urgent by competition from countries such as Japan, which are prospering by producing higher quality and lower cost goods than the rest of the world.

Clearly one solution is to achieve higher productivity (with respect to both quantity and quality) in both the manufacturing and the service sectors of the economy.

Productive efficiency is affected by many factors including government regulations, interest rates, technology, and the general wage level. In recent years increasing recognition has been given to the crucial role played by human resources in organizational productivity. A growing number of organizations are promoting human resource managers to the vice presidential level and are including them in the highest levels of corporate decision-making.

As social scientists learn more and more about how organizations can utilize their employees effectively, the potential contribution of human resource management becomes progressively greater. This book describes one important human resource technique: goal setting. As we will demonstrate, this one technique has many ramifications that bear on numerous aspects of human resource management.

Speaking generally, there is nothing original about the concept of goal setting. Everyone knows that you have to set goals in order to accomplish anything in life. Goal-directedness is, after all, the distinctive feature of rational human activity. Achieving goals is the means by which individuals achieve their own happiness, and by which organizations achieve success in the marketplace. Masuru Ibuku, the president of Sony, and Makoto Kikuchi, its director of research, have stated that Sony's success lies in the establishment of mission-oriented research and proper targets. "We find a strategy, an aim, a very real and clear *target* and then establish the necessary task forces to get the job done."* The problem, in business *and* in life, is how to use goal setting effectively.

This book is addressed to those people who are either practicing managers or who plan to become managers at some future date, and to anyone who wants to stimulate higher individual, group, or organizational performance. It focuses on the issue of how to use goal setting to improve individual and organizational productivity. But a single technique affects and is affected by many aspects of organizational life. Goal setting, for example, has implications for and is influenced by the performance appraisal system, the planning system, the feedback system, the reward system, the communication system, organizational stress, manager–subordinate relations, and union–management relations. We endeavor to show not only how and why goal setting works but also how it may be integrated with these other systems.

It should be emphasized that this is *not* a book about management by objectives (MBO) as such. Goal setting is a key element of MBO but does not have to be used as part of a formal, organization-wide program. Goal setting is useful both as a technique in its own right and as an element within a larger program that includes other motivational and organizational procedures.

*Nick Lyons, *The Sony Vision* (New York: Crown, 1976), p. 152.

Many books have been written promoting new management techniques that promise to effortlessly solve one or more perennial management problems. Some of these techniques show promise at first, only to fade away when they confront organizational realities. We believe that the usefulness of an organizational technique is shown by the test of time: has this method been proven effective over a long period? Goal setting passes this test; it has been used in organizations for at least seventy years. Only recently, however, have we learned how to use it in a truly effective manner. We hope that after reading this book you will too.

EDWIN A. LOCKE
University of Maryland
College Park, Maryland

GARY P. LATHAM
University of Washington
Seattle, Washington

Acknowledgments

We would like to thank the Office of Naval Research, who supported our work on two separate occasions. Their initial help made it possible to start our program of research on goal setting, and their later support allowed us to further develop our ideas.

The following people reviewed one or more chapters for us: Peter Belluschi, Vice President, Weyerhaeuser Company; Walter Borman, Vice President, Personnel Decision Research Institute; James Campbell, Manager of Human Resources, Scott Paper Company; Thomas Czepiel, Vice President, Scott Paper Company; Steven Hill, Director of Education and Benefits, Weyerhaeuser Company; James Lienesch, Vice President, Scott Paper Company; Barbara Rice, Personnel Manager, Natural Resources Division, Scott Paper Company; James Taylor, Industrial Relations Manager, North Pacific Paper Corporation; and John Walkush, Vice President and Mill Manager, North Pacific Paper Corporation.

Timothy Steele was very helpful in gathering material for Chapter 6. Chapter 11 was much improved as a result of numerous suggestions made by several of the individuals listed above as well as by Warren Schilit of Syracuse University (who reviewed four separate drafts), David Schweiger of the University of Houston, and Dan Power and Frank Paine of the University of Maryland.

We benefited greatly from the comments and critiques of earlier drafts of the entire manuscript by Stephen J. Carroll of the University of Maryland, Gary A. Yukl of the University of New York at Albany, and John R. Hinrichs of Management Decision Systems, Inc.

We are very grateful for the help of all these individuals. We asked them to be very critical of our early drafts of the book. Fortunately they were. The book has benefited enormously from the numerous and extensive revisions that these suggestions prompted. We should note that both of us contributed equally to the final product.

We are also very grateful to Edwin A. Locke, Jr., the senior author's father, who read the final draft of the book and made many helpful suggestions. Tom Bowden did an outstanding job of editing the entire manuscript and of compiling the index.

So many different people helped to type our manuscript that it is impossible to thank them all by name, but we are very appreciative of their hard and careful work.

1 • *What is goal setting?*

Climb high
Climb far
Your goal the sky
Your aim the star.

INSCRIPTION AT WILLIAMS COLLEGE,
WILLIAMSTOWN, MA

Much of the world's economy is in trouble. The issue facing many businesses today is nothing less than survival. Indeed, it could be argued that industry in the United States and Canada is dangerously close to being out of the game!

The Bureau of Labor Statistics published some unsettling data for 1968 to 1978.[1] Of the seven leading industrial nations, the United States ranked sixth in productivity. Canada was not included. According to the study, the rankings were:

	1968–1978 PRODUCTIVITY INCREASES
1. The Netherlands	93.7%
2. Japan	89.1
3. West Germany	63.8
4. France	61.8
5. Italy	60.1
6. United States	23.6
7. United Kingdom	21.6

1

Increasingly, top-level executives involved in strategic decision-making are beginning to emphasize the importance of an organization's *human resources* for enhancing productivity. Some have been tempted in this realm to look for quick and easy solutions. For example, sensitivity training, sometimes referred to as t-groups, was offered as the solution to most, if not all, human relations problems in the 1960s. In the 1970s, similar claims were made for job enrichment. Now employee participation under a plethora of labels is asserted to be the answer to the problem of recognizing the human side of an enterprise.

Human relations panaceas have followed a common pattern. They are first presented with a great deal of hoopla and fanfare. Exaggerated claims are made for them with little or no supporting evidence other than selected case reports. Negative outcomes or failures are not mentioned. Consequently, people in the business community rush to use them and are then shocked to find that they do not work as advertised and may even lead to harmful consequences (as in the case of t-groups). Disillusionment sets in and the popularity of the panacea rapidly declines. But when the next panacea is offered, the cycle typically starts all over again.

Unfortunately, there are no quick and easy solutions to the productivity problems faced by American business today. Since these problems have multiple causes, there must be multiple solutions. In the realm of human resource management, better selection methods must be used to match employees to organizations and to jobs. Employees must acquire and maintain the skills necessary to do their work effectively. Thus training programs need to be implemented and improved. Managers must learn techniques for conducting successful performance appraisals; and employees need to be motivated to increase the quantity and quality of their work.

Of all human resource problems, employee motivation has typically been viewed as the most mysterious and difficult to comprehend. In part, the mystery is a result of the legacy of Sigmund Freud, the founder of psychoanalysis, whose widely influential theory asserted that people were motivated fundamentally by instincts in the unconscious mind that they could neither comprehend nor control. While there is virtually no evidence for the validity of Freud's theory, motivation *is* something inside the individual. Thus it has to be inferred rather than directly observed. To thoroughly understand another person's motivation requires intensive training in psychology. Obviously, practicing managers have neither the skills nor the time to gather such information about their employees.

Fortunately, however, the practicing manager does not have to understand all the intricacies of the human psyche in order to have highly motivated employees. There is a technique that does not depend on knowledge of the employee's subconscious. This technique is not another fad or a seductive gimmick. It has been used successfully, in various forms and guises, by managers for more than seventy years. This technique is not management by objectives, although it is the basis for MBO. It is not job enrichment, but it may be the hidden element in job enrichment that is responsible for the motivational effects derived from it. The technique is not an incentive plan, but it is often associated with incentive plans and may vastly increase their effectiveness. It is not behavior modification in the historical meaning of that term, but behavior mod advocates often employ this technique successfully while using their own special terminology to describe it. It is not organizational development, but it may very well be the key to making OD interventions effective. It is not Theory X, Theory Y, or Theory Z, although it is explicitly or implicitly assumed by all three.

It is goal setting, a motivational technique that works!

Goal setting is *not* a panacea; it is not a magical solution to all management problems. It is simply an effective motivational tool that can be used by any practicing manager.

For example, goal setting is at the core of *MBO*, as the name implies. *Job enrichment* theorists advocate giving employees responsibility and freedom to do their job and, most importantly, feedback as to how well the employees are meeting their responsibilities. It is through this feedback that goals are set by employees to maintain or change their behavior. Similarly, *incentive plans* are effective to the extent that they motivate employees to set and/or accept specific, challenging organizational goals. *Behavior modification* is concerned with how the consequences of behavior reward and encourage desirable performance. In organizational settings, behavior mod practitioners typically set specific goals and then look for ways of monitoring and rewarding goal achievement.

A key premise of organizational development, Theory Y, and Theory Z is that *participation* in decision-making leads to higher work motivation than do styles of management that allow employees little or no decisional influence. This belief has turned out to be simplistic. For example, an analysis of all controlled studies of participation in organizational settings found that the average improvement in performance as a result of participation was only 0.5 percent[2]—a surprisingly low figure. It is one thing to believe that participation works and quite another to use it effectively. One discovery of our research is that participation in decision-making motivates higher performance only when higher and/or more specific goals are set than is the case without participation. If participation does not lead to the development of goals, a meeting may simply deteriorate into purposeless, unproductive get-togethers, as any manager who has suffered through such sessions can testify.

Teambuilding, a popular method of OD interventionists, is a way for a superior and subordinates together to step back, look at themselves and determine what they are doing correctly and incorrectly as a group. Such introspection or reflection is useful, however, only to the extent that the group agrees to start doing, stop doing, or continue doing specific things, i.e., to agree on specific goals.

Quality circles involve groups of peers (for instance, hourly employees) and their supervisors identifying production quality problems and discovering solutions to them. Again, this method is extremely useful for helping an organization attain its objectives, to the extent that specific action steps (goals) are recommended and implemented by the participants.

Quality of work life (QWL) generally refers to union and management representatives getting together to discuss ways of improving the work environment. Anything (for example, quality, costs, safety, or production), except collective bargaining issues, can be and usually is discussed. But enthusiasm for the procedure usually dies unless specific goals are set and steps are taken to attain them. Participation for the sake of participation, in the absence of goal setting, is often a demotivator because both management and labor quickly tire of listening to rhetoric.

Relations by objectives (RBO) refers to union and management officials together establishing common goals as to how they can all work together effectively under the existing labor contract. Like MBO, goal setting is inherent in the process.

Now let us discuss the *technique* of goal setting. As noted above, goal setting is not new. It was used at the turn of the century by Frederick W. Taylor, the founder of scientific management. He called it *task management.* Some of Taylor's ideas evolved into the technique of management by objectives, which has goal setting as its core.[3] However, goal setting does not have to be part of a wider management system in order to be effective. It can be applied to an individual employee, to work groups, or to managers, as well as to the organization as a whole.

A *goal* is what an employee is trying to accomplish on the job. It is the object or aim of an action. There are many familiar concepts that are similar in meaning to that of goal; e.g., *task:* a piece of work to be accomplished; *performance standard:* a measuring rod for evaluating performance (usually referring to a minimum acceptable amount or quality); *quota:* an assigned amount of work or production; *work norm:* a standard of acceptable conduct as defined by a work group; *objective:* the ultimate aim of an action; *deadline:* a time limit for accomplishing some task; and *budget:* a spending limit for an individual, project, department, or organization.

In most instances, the distinctions between these concepts are not of great importance; thus we use the word goal as an umbrella term. No distinction is made, for example, between the terms goal and objective. This is because both of these concepts have the same two elements in common: they imply or specify a *direction* for action to take, and they imply a specified *amount* or quality of work to be accomplished.

The principle of goal setting is recognized implicitly or explicitly by virtually all major theories of and approaches to work motivation.[4] It is no accident that the principle of goal setting is so pervasive; it constitutes a recognition of a basic fact about rational human action, namely, that it is naturally purposeful. However, since individuals possess free will (volition), it is not inevitable that every individual *will* set goals. People have a choice in this regard—not only with respect to whether they set goals, but also as to the types of goals they will set (number, complexity, time span), the process by which they will set them, and their integration with other organizational practices.

Now consider the evidence that goal setting *works*. In addition to the fact that goal setting has been used by managers for more than seventy years, there have been more than 110 goal setting experiments conducted in laboratory and organizational settings in just the past twelve years. Ninety percent of these studies obtained positive results for goal setting. This makes goal setting one of the most dependable and robust techniques in all the motivational literature.[5] A recent study of factors causing high and low productivity in one plant of a multinational corporation found that goal setting and related events (e.g., deadlines) were the single most frequently mentioned cause of incidents of high productivity.[6] In another company, the use of goal setting with a single work group saved $250,000.[7] It has now been more than eight years since goal setting was introduced in this group and the goals continue to be effective to this day. Considering all published studies of goal setting in organizations, we find that it has led to a median improvement in performance (i.e., quantity of output, quality of output, etc.) of 16 percent with a range of 2 percent to 57.5 percent.[8]

Goal setting has been found to be effective with both union and nonunion employees, blacks and whites, males and females, the young and the old, as well as the highly educated and the poorly educated—in short, it works on people! Studies of goal setting have involved dozens of different tasks including logging, typing, energy conservation, clerical work, computation, scientific and engineering work, training, machine servicing, managing and supervision, production work, technician's work, keypunching, performance evaluation, sales, telephone service work, truck loading, ship loading, die casting, safety behaviors of pastry workers, customer service, foremen's work, pulpwood production, and assembly work. Although, as we shall see, the complexity of the task does affect the way one should go about setting goals, there is no evidence that there are tasks on which goal setting fails to work, providing that employees have control over what they do.

In short, goals can be set for virtually any action or outcome that is verifiable or measurable; and since anything that exists, exists in a certain amount and is therefore in principle measurable, goal setting is almost universally applicable. This is not to say that measuring performance is necessarily easy. For example, it is much easier to measure the quality of a typed letter than the quality of a research proposal to study the mechanisms of cancer or the quality of a middle-level executive's performance (when he or she has only partial control over the outcomes of the work). Nevertheless, the quality of a research proposal or of a manager's performance can be measured if sufficient effort and thought are spent on the problem.

You may wonder at this point, if goal setting is such an effective and natural technique, why it is necessary to write a book about it. Why can't I just do it on my own? The answer to the question is simply this: *it is not self-evident how to set goals effectively.* Like every other skill that we possess, the skill of goal setting must be acquired. For example, one could argue that all employees have goals in some sense of the word, but these goals may be vague, confusing, conflicting, unchallenging, impossible, meaningless, or unrelated to an organization's objectives. When this is the case, the goals do not bring about or sustain effective performance. It could also be argued that, since goal setting is a known technique, it is already used systematically throughout virtually all organizations. This simply is not so. In fact, the systematic and effective use of goal setting is the exception rather than the rule in most organizations primarily because most managers do not know enough about the goal setting process. We hope that this book will provide them with such knowledge.

The question of what benefits managers can expect from goal setting is answered in Chapter 2. Why does goal setting work? This is explained in Chapter 3. How should you actually go about setting goals? Chapter 4 is devoted to a detailed explanation of steps to follow. How do you insure goal commitment? A variety of techniques are described in Chapter 5. What practices and procedures are needed to implement goal setting effectively? Chapter 6 is devoted to this issue. How can goal setting be used in performance appraisal? The positive effects of setting goals during appraisal sessions are described in Chapter 7. In Chapter 8 we discuss the relationship between goal setting and stress, and how unnecessary stress can be avoided. The relationships between goal setting and other motivational techniques and devices (such as money, job enrichment, participation, and behavior modification) are explained in Chapter 9. Can you use goal setting with unionized workers? The answer is "yes," if you follow the crucial guidelines given in Chapter 10. What about strategic goal setting? Is there anything that distinguishes strategic goals from other types of goals? Again the answer is "yes," and the distinctions are explained in Chapter 11. Finally, are there dangers and pitfalls in goal setting? If so, what are they and how can they be guarded against or overcome? This subject is treated in Chapter 12.

When you have finished this book, you will see why and how goal setting works. You will be able to make it work yourself.

SUMMARY

Organizations need to find ways of increasing their productivity, quality, and efficiency. This requires a multifaceted approach. One key approach is to maximize the use of the organization's human resources. This can be done only with human resource techniques that have proven to be effective against the test of time. Goal setting is one such technique. Its effects are reliable, powerful, and durable and are applicable to people throughout the organization performing a wide variety of tasks. The purpose of this book is to show the practicing manager how to use goal setting effectively.

2 • The benefits of goal setting*

Although the technique of goal setting has been used for more than seventy years, it has been only in the last two decades that behavioral scientists have begun to study it systematically through the use of controlled experiments. Our own program of research on goal setting has been going on for more than eighteen years and is still continuing. The following is a summary of what we have found.

LABORATORY AND FIELD RESEARCH

Our research program began in the laboratory. In a series of experiments, individuals were assigned different types of goals on a variety of straightforward tasks—numerical addition, brainstorming, assembling toys. Repeatedly it was found that people who were assigned difficult goals performed better than did those who were assigned moderately difficult or easy goals. Furthermore, individuals who had specific, challenging goals outperformed those who were given vague goals such as "do your best." Finally, we observed that performance feedback led to improved performance only when these incentives led individuals to set goals for improving their performance.

*This chapter is based in part on our article entitled, "Goal Setting: A Motivational Technique that Works," *Organizational Dynamics*, 1979, Vol. 8, 68–80. Reprinted by permission of the publisher, AMACOM, a division of American Management Association.

While these results were consistently replicated in the laboratory, there was no proof that they could be applied to actual work settings. Fortunately, just as Locke published a summary of the laboratory studies in 1968, Latham began a separate series of experiments in the wood products industry that demonstrated the practical application of these findings. These field studies did not start out as a test of a laboratory theory but rather as a response to a specific productivity problem.

In the late 1960s, six member companies of the American Pulpwood Association became concerned about increasing the productivity of independent loggers in the south. These loggers were entrepreneurs on whom multimillion-dollar companies depended for most of their raw material. The problem was twofold. First, these entrepreneurs did not work for a single company; they worked for themselves. Thus they were free to (and often did) work erratic hours; for example, two days during one week, four days during a second week, five half-days during a third week, or whatever other schedule they preferred. In short, these workers could be classified as marginal because their attendance as well as their production were considered to be highly unsatisfactory by conventional company standards. Second, the major approach taken to alleviate this difficulty had been to develop equipment that would make the industry less dependent on this type of worker. A limitation of this approach was that many logging supervisors were unable to obtain the financing necessary to purchase even a small tractor, let alone a rubber-tired skidder used to haul timber.

Consequently, we designed a survey that would help managers determine "what makes these people tick."[1] The survey was conducted orally in the field with 292 supervisors of these independent logging operations. Complex statistical analyses of the data identified three basic types of supervisors. One type stayed on the job with the workers, gave them instructions and explanations, trained them, read the trade magazines, and had little difficulty financing the equipment they needed. The productivity of their units, however, was average at best.

The operation of the second group of supervisors was slightly less mechanized. These supervisors provided little training for their work force. They simply drove their employees to the woods, gave them a specific daily or weekly production goal, left them alone each day unsupervised, and returned at night to take them home. Labor turnover was high and productivity was again average.

The operation of the third group of supervisors was relatively unmechanized. These leaders stayed on the job with the workers, trained them, gave instructions and explanations, and, in addition, set a specific production goal for the day or week. Not only was each crew's productivity high, as defined by cords per employee hour, but their injury rate was well below average.

These results suggest two conclusions. First, mechanization alone will not increase the productivity of logging crews. Just as the average taxpayer would probably commit more mathematical errors if he or she were to use a computer in order to complete an income tax return, the average logger misuses, and frequently abuses, the equipment he purchases (for example, driving a skidder with two flat tires or failing to change the oil filter). This increases not only the logger's downtime but also his costs, which, in turn, can force him out of business. The second conclusion of the survey was that setting a specific production goal combined with the presence of a supervisor to ensure goal commitment brings about a significant increase in productivity.

These conclusions were greeted by the six companies who sponsored this research with the standard, but valid, cliché, "Statistics don't prove causation." Our comments regarding the value of machinery were especially irritating to managers in these companies, many of whom had earned degrees in engineering. Consequently, the Georgia Kraft Company decided to replicate the survey in order to check our findings.

The company's study placed each of 892 independent logging supervisors into one of three categories, based on the types of supervisors our previous survey had identified, namely, (1) stays on the job but does not set specific production goals; (2) sets specific production goals but does not stay on the job; and (3) stays on the job and sets specific production goals.

Once again, goal setting, in combination with the on-site presence of a supervisor, was shown to be the key to improving productivity.

TESTING FOR THE HAWTHORNE EFFECT

Management may have been unfamiliar with different theories of motivation, but it was fully aware of one label—the Hawthorne effect, which states that attention by itself can increase productivity. Managers in these wood products companies remained unconvinced that anything so simple as staying on the job with the men and setting a specific production goal could have an appreciable effect on productivity. They pointed out that the results simply reflected the positive effects any supervisor would have on the work unit after giving his or her crew attention. And they were unimpressed by the laboratory experiments we cited, experiments showing that individuals who have specific, hard goals solve more arithmetic problems or assemble more Tinker Toys than do people who are told "do your best."

But by the early 1970s the country's economic picture made it critical to continue the study of inexpensive techniques to improve employee motivation and productivity. We were granted permission to run one more project to test the effectiveness of goal setting.[2]

Twenty independent logging crews who were nearly identical in size, mechanization level, type of terrain worked, productivity, and employee attendance were located. The logging supervisors of these crews were in the habit of staying on the job with their crews, but they did not set production goals. Half the crews were randomly selected to receive training in goal setting; the remaining crews served as a control group, receiving no training.

The logging supervisors who were to set goals were told that we had found a way to increase productivity at no financial expense to anyone. To the ten supervisors in the training group we gave production tables developed through time-and-motion studies by the company's engineers. These tables made it possible to determine how much wood should be harvested during a given number of employee-hours worked. The supervisors were then asked to use these tables as a guide in determining a specific production goal to assign each employee. In addition, each sawhand was given a tally-meter (counter) that could be worn on the belt; the sawhand was asked to punch the counter each time a tree was felled. Finally, permission was requested to measure the crew's performance on a weekly basis.

The ten supervisors in the control group—those who were not asked to set production goals—were told that we were interested in learning the extent to which productivity is affected by absenteeism and injuries. They were urged to "do their best" to maximize the crew's productivity and attendance and to minimize injuries. We explained that the data we would be collecting would hopefully be useful in determining ways to increase productivity at little or no cost to them.

To control for the Hawthorne effect, we made an equal number of visits to the control group and the training group. Performance was measured for twelve weeks. During this time, the productivity of the goal setting group was significantly higher than that of the control group. Moreover, attendance was significantly higher in the crews that set goals than in the crews who were simply urged to do their best. Injury and turnover rates were low in both groups.

This study was of immediate importance to the logging industry because it demonstrated a relatively simple method for increasing productivity, one that did not require a large capital outlay such as the purchase of expensive machinery. All that was required was for the logging supervisor to provide on-the-job supervision and modify the policy of "doing the best I can" to include a daily or weekly production goal.

A third study was conducted with unionized truck drivers (see Chapter 10) who were not loading their trucks to maximum capacity.[3] A nine-month goal setting project with these drivers saved the company $250,000. This figure, determined by the company's accountants, is based on the cost of additional trucks that would have been required to deliver the same quantity of logs to the mill if goal setting had not been implemented.

The dollars-saved figure is even higher when the cost of the additional diesel fuel that would have been consumed and the expenses that would have been incurred in recruiting and hiring additional truck drivers are factored in.

Taken together, these studies demonstrated that goal setting in industry worked just as well as it did in the laboratory. Specific, challenging goals led to better performance than easy or vague goals such as "do your best," and feedback motivated higher performance only when it led to the setting of higher goals.

A representative sample of the results of field studies of goal setting are shown in Table 1. Each of these ten studies compared the performance of employees who were given

Table 1 · Representative Field Studies of Goal Setting

RESEARCHER(S)	TASK	DURATION OF STUDY OR OF SIGNIFICANT EFFECTS	PERCENT OF CHANGE IN PERFORMANCE[a]
Blumenfield & Leidy	Servicing soft drink coolers	Unspecified	+27
Dockstader	Keypunching	3 mos.	+27
Ivancevich	Skilled technical jobs	9 mos.	+15
Ivancevich	Sales	9 mos.	+24
Kim & Hamner	5 telephone service jobs	3 mos.	+13
Latham & Baldes	Loading trucks	9 mos.[b]	+26
Latham & Yukl	Logging	2 mos.	+18
Latham & Yukl	Typing	5 weeks	+11
Migliore	Mass production	2 years	+16
Umstot, Bell, & Mitchell	Coding land parcels	1–2 days[c]	+16

[a]Percentage changes were obtained by subtracting pre-goal setting performance from post-goal setting performance and dividing by pre-goal setting performance. Different experimental groups were combined where appropriate. If a control group was available, the percentage figure represents the difference of the percentage changes between the experimental and control groups. If multiple performance measures were used, the median improvement on all measures was used. The authors would like to thank Dena Feren and Vicki McCaleb for performing these calculations.
[b]Performance has remained high for eight years.
[c]Simulated organization.

SOURCE: Locke and Latham, "Goal Setting: A Motivational Technique That Works," *Organizational Dynamics*, 1979, Vol. 8, 75. Reprinted, by permission of the publisher, from *Organizational Dynamics*, Autumn 1979. © 1979 by AMACOM, a division of American Management Associations. All rights reserved.

specific challenging goals with those who were either told to "do your best" or else were not given any goals. Note that goal setting has been successful across a wide variety of jobs and industries. The effects of goal setting have been recorded for as long as eight years after the onset of the program, although the results of most studies that employed rigorous scientific procedures generally lasted at most a few weeks or months before goal setting was more widely implemented in the company. The median improvement in performance in the ten studies shown in Table 1 was 16 percent.

A CRITICAL INCIDENTS STUDY

To explore further the importance of goal setting in organizations, a study was conducted in two plants of a high technology, multinational corporation on the East Coast.[4] Seventy-one engineers, fifty managers, and thirty-one clerks were asked to describe a specific instance when they were especially productive and when they were especially unproductive on their present jobs. Of primary interest here are the external events perceived by employees as being responsible for the high-productivity and low-productivity incidents. The results are shown in Table 2.

The first set of events—pursuing a specific goal, having a large amount of work, working under a deadline, or having an uninterrupted routine—accounted for more than half the high-productivity events. Similarly, the converse of these—goal blockage, having a small amount of work, lacking a deadline, and suffering work interruptions—accounted for nearly 60 percent of the low-productivity events. Note that the first set of categories are all relevant to goal setting and the second set point to either a lack of goals or to goal blockage. The goal category itself—that of pursuing an attainable goal or goal blockage—was the one most frequently used to describe both high- and low-productivity incidents.

The next four categories—which are pertinent to Frederick Herzberg's theory of job enrichment—are task interest, responsibility, promotion, and recognition. These categories are

Table 2 • Events Perceived As Causing High and Low Productivity[a]

EVENT	PERCENT OF TIMES EVENT CAUSED	
	HIGH PRODUCTIVITY	LOW PRODUCTIVITY
Goal pursuit/Goal blockage	17.1	23.0
Large amount of work/Small amount of work	12.5	19.0
Deadline or schedule/No deadline	15.1	3.3
Smooth work routine/Interrupted routine	5.9	14.5
Total	50.6	59.8
Interesting task/Uninteresting task	17.1	11.2
Increased responsibility/Decreased responsibility	13.8	4.6
Anticipated promotion/Promotion denied	1.3	0.7
Verbal recognition/Criticism	4.6	2.6
Total	36.8	19.1
Pleasant personal relationships/ Unpleasant personal relationships	10.5	9.9
Anticipated pay increase/Pay increase denied	1.3	1.3
Pleasant working conditions/ Unpleasant working conditions	0.7	0.7
Other (miscellaneous)	—	9.3
Total	12.5	21.2

[a]Based on 152 respondents.

SOURCE: Locke and Latham, "Goal Setting: A Motivational Technique That Works," *Organizational Dynamics*, 1979, Vol. 8, 76. Reprinted, by permission of the publisher, from *Organizational Dynamics*, Autumn 1979. © 1979 by AMACOM, a division of American Management Associations. All rights reserved.

less important, accounting for 36.8 percent of the high-productivity incidents (the opposite of these four categories accounting for 19.1 percent of the lows). The remaining categories were less important still.

Employees were also asked to identify the responsible agent behind the events that had led to high and low productivity. In both cases, the employees themselves, their immediate supervisors, and the organization were the agents most frequently mentioned.

The concept of goal setting is a very simple one. Interestingly, however, we have heard two contradictory types of reaction when the idea was introduced to managers. Some have claimed it was so simple and self-evident that everyone, including they themselves, already used it. This, we have found, is not true. Time after time we have heard the following response from subordinates after goal setting was introduced: "We always had a general idea of where we were headed and what was required of us, but this clarifies for the first time exactly what we are expected to do." Conversely, other managers have argued that the idea would not work, precisely *because* it is so simple (implying that something more radical and complex was needed). Again, results have proved them wrong.

HOW IS GOAL SETTING BENEFICIAL?

Our research program has demonstrated that the most reliable effect of goal setting is to *raise productivity* or *improve work quality* (see Chapter 1). However, there are a variety of other beneficial consequences as well.

Goals, for example, help *clarify expectations*. Even engineers and scientists have reported that the setting of specific goals made it clear to them for the first time what line managers and their own supervisors wanted them to do.[5]

Goals can also *relieve boredom*.[6] Consider, for example, the job of logging in the southern United States. Harvesting pulpwood can be a monotonous, tiring job with little or no inherent interest for many workers. Introducing a goal that is difficult but attainable increases the challenge of the job and provides a sense of purpose. The same is true for numerous other jobs.

When goals are attained and feedback is provided indicating that these goals have been reached, employees feel a sense of *increased liking* for the task and *satisfaction with their performance* and the work they are doing.[7] Feedback regarding goal accomplishment provides the employee with *recognition* by both peers and supervisors or managers. Such feedback and recognition may induce *spontaneous competition* among employees, which further enhances their performance.[8]

Goal setting is not only effective with scientists, managers, and educated blue collar workers; it also works with minorities. Uneducated black workers in the south have reported feelings of greater *self-confidence, pride* in achievement, and increased *willingness* to accept future challenges as a result of goal setting. This is not surprising in light of research conducted for the Equal Employment Opportunity Commission.[9] This research showed that culturally and educationally disadvantaged individuals are often characterized by weak ego development, a lack of self-confidence, and a negative self-concept. Moreover, these individuals frequently have had little experience in receiving recognition for success in a learning task. The cycle of skill mastery in which successful experiences generate more motivation to perform, which in turn guarantees levels of skill sufficient to prevent discouragement and so on, is typically reversed for these individuals.

Goal setting, especially participative goal setting, has been found to be effective in increasing performance and generating feelings of competency among these employees.[10] The setting of a specific goal made it clear to these workers what was required of them. Participation in setting the goal provided them with the confidence that they could attain it.

SUMMARY

An eighteen-year program of research was started in the laboratory and then continued in organizational settings. The same results were obtained in both cases. People who are given specific, challenging goals perform better than people who are given specific, easy goals, vague goals (such as "do your best"), or no goals. Critical-incident studies have shown that goal setting can be a key determinant of high productivity. In addition to improving productivity, goal setting may also clarify expectations, relieve boredom, increase task liking and satisfaction with performance, lead to increased recognition and spontaneous competition, and increase confidence and pride in one's work.

3 • Why does goal setting work?

Imagine that you have just been hired by a small oil company as Vice President in Charge of Exploration. Assume that you are told, "It's your job to explore." At this point you would have a general idea of what you were supposed to do. You would know, for example, that you should be concerned with exploration rather than with personnel, finance, or marketing. Even so, you would still have many unanswered questions. Where should you look? What is your budget? How soon do you need results? How many exploratory wells can be drilled?

All these questions could be answered by specifying the objective more precisely. For example, rather than just being told to "explore," you could be told, "Look for new properties in Oklahoma and Texas. We need to develop three producing wells in the next year, which means you may need to drill up to six exploratory wells. Your budget is $10 million."

Observe that this objective is much more specific than the first one and therefore directs your actions much more precisely. For example, exploration is limited to only two states. The number of wells is specified. A time frame is included, and a budget is provided.

The principle here is that *specific goals direct action more reliably than vague or general goals*. The most effective way to make goals specific is to specify the activities to be performed or the results to be obtained in quantitative terms, e.g., "drill three new wells" rather than "drill wells"; "do it in one year" rather than "do it as soon as you can"; "limit spending to $10 million" rather than "be frugal."

Quantification should be done with respect to any aspect of performance that can be measured. Quantification reduces ambiguity by allowing less leeway for individual interpretation. For example, one executive's interpretation of frugal (e.g., spend $35 million) might be very different from another's (e.g., spend $10 million). Increasing goal specificity reduces the probability of misunderstandings between a middle manager and a vice president or between a middle manager and subordinates. *Goal specificity results in clear expectations.* As one formerly frustrated engineer put it after a new goal-based performance appraisal system was established, "This is the first time in twelve years that I know just what that SOB expects of me."

There is another mechanism by which goals affect performance. Compare the goal of developing three producing wells in the next year with the goal of producing six producing wells in the same time span. The two objectives are equally specific but one is harder than the other. Thus, goals can differ with respect to difficulty as well as specificity. Extensive research based on more than fifty studies has established that, within reasonable limits, *the harder or more challenging the goal, the better the resulting performance.*[1] This relationship is shown in Section A of Figure 1.

A hard goal leads to greater performance than an easy or moderate goal because, given that the goal is accepted, people try harder to attain the hard goal. They exert more effort, they show fewer lapses of attention or performance, and they work faster.[2] In short, people become motivated in proportion to the level of the challenge with which they are faced. The only alternative is to reject the challenge, a problem we will deal with in Chapter 5.

On the other side of the coin, when goals are less challenging, performance is lower. One large consumer products company, for example, had as its goal the doubling of profits every ten years. In terms of real growth and stock value, this company had been in the doldrums for many years. Its earnings growth had not kept pace with inflation, and its stock had

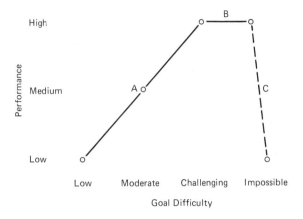

A: Performance of committed individuals with adequate ability
B: Performance of committed individuals who are working at capacity
C: Performance of individuals who lack commitment to high goals

Figure 1 • Relation of Goal Difficulty to Task Performance

dropped 40 percent within an eight-year period. The company had a history of using slow, cautious, low-risk business strategies that often allowed competitors to steal markets in which its own products could have been dominant.[3] According to goal setting theory, this company was achieving exactly what it deserved: it was setting very modest goals and it was achieving very modest results. In our opinion, a turnaround would have required the setting of a much harder goal (e.g., doubling profits every five years) and the development of innovative strategies to attain them.

Compare this overly cautious procedure with that of the multimillionaire, Curt Carlson, owner of Carlson Companies, which includes interests in catalogue showrooms, restaurants, hotels, and imports:

> He created a stir [in 1975] . . . by announcing that the company was aiming for $1 billion in annual sales by 1981, more than double the sales figure at the time. As things are turning out, Carlson Cos., skeptics not withstanding, is well ahead of schedule; it will hit the $1 billion mark [in 1978].[4]

As we stressed earlier, specific, challenging goals consistently lead to better performance than the goal of "doing one's best."[5] This is because, paradoxically, people do not do their best when they are trying to do their best! "Doing your best" is a vague goal because the meaning of "best" is not specified. The way to get individuals to truly do their best is to set a challenging, quantitative goal that demands the maximum use of their skills and abilities.

At some point, of course, people reach the limit of their capacities so that, even with great effort, their performance does not improve. This situation is shown in Section B of Figure 1. Note that performance does not necessarily decline when goals are too difficult to reach, providing that the individual is still trying for the goal or at least trying to get as close to it as possible. For example, if your objective is to reduce operating costs by 40 percent and this proves impossible, and if you keep trying anyway, you might be able to reduce costs by 35 percent—still better than no reduction, or a reduction of 10, 20, or 30 percent.

Thus partial success can be an effective substitute for complete success, especially if due credit is given for it. Experiencing partial success can be enhanced by providing individuals with subgoals representing steps leading to the attainment of an overall goal. Subgoals are especially useful when the overall goal is long-term.

It is conceivable, of course, that a goal could be perceived as so hard that an individual would not only give up trying to reach it, but would even give up trying to get close to it. Total apathy could result, as shown by the dotted line (Section C) of Figure 1.

The evidence indicates that challenging goals are most likely to lead to lower commitment and thus to lower performance in two circumstances: (1) when the employee or manager is generally lacking in self-confidence[6], and (2) when partial success is either impossible or meaningless. For example, it has been found that if employees are under a *task and bonus* system, in which they receive a monetary bonus only for succeeding in reaching a goal, performance drops when the goal is seen as very hard or impossible to reach.[7] Since partial success brings *no* payment rather than partial payment, people give up if they think they cannot attain the goal. In contrast, under a *piece-rate* system, in which payment is *proportional* to performance (regardless of whether the goal is fully attained), performance increases as the goals become more difficult. This finding is shown in Figure 2. Note that with easy or moderate goals, the task and bonus system is superior to the piece-rate system. All-or-none rewards work well when people are sure the goals can be reached.

There is also a danger in setting goals at too low a level. Once reached, the goals may become performance ceilings and thus inhibit further improvement even when it is possible. This brings up a third mechanism by which goal setting improves performance: *persistence*. Persistence involves directed effort extended through time.

Continuing with the earlier example, if within eight months you had succeeded in developing three operating oil wells while your goal was six within one year, you would continue to work at the task rather than easing up since you would not yet have attained your objective. In contrast, if your goal had been only three, you would probably slack off for the rest of the year, unless a new goal were set. Given goal commitment,

Figure 2 • Relation of Goal Difficulty to Performance Under Piece-Rate and Task and Bonus Incentives

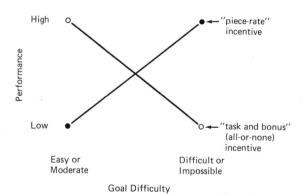

SOURCE: Based on John C. Mowen, R. Dennis Middlemist, and David Luther, "Joint Effects of Assigned Goal Level and Incentive Structure on Task Performance: A Laboratory Study," *Journal of Applied Psychology*, 1981, Vol. 66, 598–603.

action does not cease until and unless the goal is reached, or reached to the maximum extent possible. Easy goals result in a shorter duration of effort and attention than hard goals.[8]

The underlying motivation here is that people gain a sense of accomplishment and efficacy from attaining goals. They enjoy the sense of completion or *closure* that comes with completion of a task. Thus, assuming a reasonable degree of commitment, there is a feeling of discomfort when a job is not finished—the tension of an unfulfilled purpose. There is a drive to keep going until the goal is reached. A classic example is engineer Jim Guyer of Data General Corporation, a member of a team trying desperately to design a radically new minicomputer in record time. Often he would work as late as 3 A.M. as a result of his total absorption in the project: "I would start sniffing something around ten-thirty at night, and I just *could not* let go."[9]

The above three mechanisms—direction, effort, and persistence—are relatively straightforward in their effects on performance. Faced with a specific, challenging task or goal, people direct their efforts in line with what is required to reach the goal until it is attained or until they get as close to it as they can. Goal attainment depends on the individual's use of existing skills and knowledge combined with the determination to use that knowledge.

In many cases, however, especially with managerial jobs, the best way to attain a given goal is not known in advance. Although executives must use their existing skills, they may not know precisely what to do in a given situation because the circumstances are unique. In certain respects, every decision situation has unique elements. For example, if the objective is to find six new oil wells, even the most experienced and knowledgeable executive will not know exactly where to drill, how deep to drill, how much oil will be found, or what kinds of problems will be discovered once the drilling starts.

To achieve the goal of finding six oil-producing wells, an appropriate strategy or plan of action will have to be developed. The goal motivates the development of a strategy, but the content of the strategy is not specified by the goal—it must be discovered through planning, problem-solving, and decision-making.

Generally, the higher the level of the job, the more complex the tasks, and therefore the greater the need to discover appropriate strategies for goal attainment. This is especially the case when there are multiple goals for a single job. Not only does a plan have to be developed to attain each goal, but these plans must be integrated so that attaining one goal does not negate or prevent the attainment of another.

For example, as Vice President in Charge of Exploration, you would have to develop plans for doing geological surveys and interpreting the results, pricing land for possible purchase, buying or renting drill rigs, finding suitable employees to man the drill rigs, determining how long to drill in a given spot, making best use of the available funds, obtaining permits from various levels of government, and so on. These plans would have to be tied together so that, for example, enough money was available both to purchase promising sites and to pay for equipment and crew wages when a promising drilling site was discovered.

The most complex strategies will usually be required for goals in the realm of strategic planning since such goals must encompass the entire organization (see Chapter 11). Again goal setting is valuable because it provides the impetus to develop appropriate strategies.

Few people have identified the overall benefits of goal setting better than former General Motors President Alfred P. Sloan who revealed that his "guiding principle was to make our standards difficult to achieve, but possible to attain which I believe is the most effective way of capitalizing on the initiative, resourcefulness, and capabilities of operating personnel." [10]

SUMMARY

Goals facilitate performance in four ways: they direct attention and action, they mobilize energy and effort, they increase persistence, and they motivate the development of appropriate task strategies. Goals are most effective in producing high performance when they are both specific and challenging. Even goals that cannot be fully reached will lead to high effort levels, provided that partial success can be achieved and is rewarded. The motivation to attain long-range goals can be facilitated by the setting of shorter-term subgoals.

4 • *How to set goals*

In this chapter we discuss how goals should be set. Effective goal setting is not difficult, but there are at least seven key steps that need to be followed in order to obtain optimal results.

1. Specify the general objective or tasks to be done.   What do you want to accomplish? Do you want to discover oil properties? Reduce costs? Increase sales? Enhance work quality on an assembly line? Improve customer service? Develop subordinates? The number of possibilities is nearly limitless—there can be as many goals as there are jobs or employees. And since a given employee generally performs several different tasks, typically there will be even more goals than there are jobs. A useful way to specify an employee's tasks is to begin with a general job description.

A job description should indicate what an employee is expected to do, that is, what tasks are to be performed, what outcome the employee is responsible for obtaining, what deadlines are to be met, what other jobs this job is to be coordinated with, what equipment is to be used, what supervisory responsibilities are involved, and so on. Some job descriptions list the *critical* job requirements, that is, requirements that make the difference between success (if fulfilled) and failure (if not fulfilled).

2. Specify how the performance in question will be measured.   Obviously some actions or outcomes are easier to measure than others. For example, it is usually easy to measure sales in dollar volume or number of units sold. The performance of typists can be measured by counting the number of words typed, the number of errors made, and/or the time spent on each job. The performance of truck drivers can be measured by counting the number of trips made each day. And records can be kept of the time required by clerks to answer customer inquiries.

Typically, work outcomes are measured by one of three standards:

> Physical units, e.g., quantity of production, market share, number of errors, number of rejects (quality control), and so forth;
>
> Time, e.g., meeting deadlines, servicing customers, completing a project, coming to work each day, being punctual, and the like;
>
> Money, e.g., profits, sales, costs, budgets, debts, income, and so on

Sometimes, however, it is difficult to obtain valid measures of the work outcomes of a single individual. This may be because to do so would be too costly or because the outcomes are determined by factors beyond the control of the employee in question.

An alternative in such a case is to measure the *behaviors* or *actions* that are assumed to lead to successful outcomes (insofar as these are under the control of the employee). Such an approach again begins with a job analysis, which, as noted above, may specify only the critical actions necessary for performing a job satisfactorily (e.g., for a foreman: "plans work so that subordinates are not kept waiting for needed materials"; for a personnel manager: "does manpower planning so that when an employee quits or retires, a replacement is readily available"). These actions are typically discovered by questioning a representative sample of job incumbents and their peers, supervisors, subordinates, and clients (as applicable). From this list Behavioral Observation Scales (BOS) can then be developed.[1] A sample scale for the job of manager is shown in Figure 3.

Figure 3 · Example of One BOS Criterion or Performance Dimension for Evaluating Managers

---

1. Overcoming Resistance to Change
    (1) Gives the details of the change to subordinates.
        Almost Never 0 1 2 3 4 Almost Always
    (2) Explains why the change is needed.
        Almost Never 0 1 2 3 4 Almost Always
    (3) Explains how the change will affect the employee.
        Almost Never 0 1 2 3 4 Almost Always
    (4) Listens to the employee's concerns.
        Almost Never 0 1 2 3 4 Almost Always
    (5) Asks the employee for assistance in making the change work.
        Almost Never 0 1 2 3 4 Almost Always
    (6) If necessary, specifies the date for a follow-up meeting to discuss/resolve the employee's concerns.
        Almost Never 0 1 2 3 4 Almost Always

TOTAL = _____

BELOW ADEQUATE[a]	ADEQUATE	FULL	EXCELLENT	SUPERIOR
0–5	6–10	11–15	16–19	20–24

---

[a]Score categories are set by management.

Once BOS are developed, goals can be set based on the frequency with which the individual being rated demonstrates or engages in these actions. Studies have shown that on jobs where job performance can be measured in terms of physical units (e.g., quantity of production), such measures correlate significantly with ratings of the same individuals on BOS. This finding is not surprising. After all, in order to produce, the individual has to do something. Thus, one has the option of measuring the final outcome (if available) or the actions that brought about the outcome (BOS) depending on which is more feasible or meaningful. Action or behavioral scales not only facilitate the setting of goals or performance standards, but they also help to pinpoint the strategies that need to be followed to attain high performance.

3. Specify the standard or target to be reached. This involves not only using the quantitative scale established in step 2 above but also indicating the specific *degree* of performance to be achieved; for example, producing sixty units per hour, attaining a 1 percent lower reject rate, completing the project by May

1, answering all customer queries within twenty-four hours, increasing profits by ten percent, increasing sales by twenty-five percent, cutting costs by 3 percent, etc. If BOS are used, the goal might be "scoring 20 or higher out of a possible 24 points on the scale."

Note that formulating the goal in this manner satisfies the criterion of *specificity* noted in the previous chapter. The *challenge* criterion can be met by insuring that the goal is set at a sufficiently high level.

There are numerous ways to set specific targets depending on the context and the purpose for which the targets will be used. For routine, repetitive jobs, the most scientifically precise methods of setting goals are the *time-and-motion study techniques* made famous in the early 1900s by Frederick W. Taylor and Frank B. Gilbreth.[2] Motion study involves studying the job with the intention of eliminating all unnecessary or wasted motions and simplifying necessary ones. Time study, which logically follows motion study, involves timing a work cycle repeatedly in order to determine the average time taken to complete it by one or more competent employees who have been instructed on how to perform the proper motions. The time is then prorated across the working day with allowances for fatigue, set-up time, and various interruptions. From this calculation an expected day's production can be determined. By measuring unit times only on "first class workmen," Taylor insured that the resulting target or *task* was challenging. Taylor's technique made it possible for the first time in history to determine objectively, within a reasonably small range of error, a "fair day's work."

To take a specific example, consider the procedures used by APA Transport Corporation in North Bergen, New Jersey. This company ranks eighty-fifth in gross operating revenues among trucking companies but ranks first in operating ratio (operating expenses divided by revenues). Despite the fact that the employees are unionized and the company is located in a high cost-of-living area, they control costs by setting explicit standards for their drivers based on extensive time studies of the drivers' tasks, loads, and routes. Standard times are calculated for each run, and the drivers are given feedback from a computer printout daily showing their performance in relation to the standards. The standards are met 96 percent of the time. Consistent with Taylor's philosophy, the company only hires "first class" drivers, using a rigorous screening process. [3]

While time-and-motion study is now accepted as a standard industrial engineering technique, it is not always well-received by employees, especially in cases where job changes lead to retiming of jobs that are paid on incentive wages. Standards may end up being tighter than before. The result is often that employees are asked to work harder for the same amount of pay—a practice that is equivalent to rate-cutting. To prevent this, employees sometimes try to fool the time study engineers by adding unnecessary motions or misadjusting their machines, and the like. The engineers in turn know they are being fooled and try to compensate for it. Thus, time-and-motion study can become a battle of wits between management and labor[4], especially when there is lack of mutual trust.[5]

Taylor recommended that time study be done very carefully at the outset and that rates never be cut once they are established. Unfortunately, his recommendations have not always been followed, and thus suspicion of and resistance to time-and-motion study are common among workers. While this can be overcome by management policies that encourage trust on the part of employees (e.g., no rate-cutting, no layoffs), such policies take time to implement.

A more immediately acceptable, if less scientifically precise, way to set goals is to use *previous performance* as a standard. Most employees consider their average previous performance (or that of the group or plant) to be a fair and reasonable goal. There is the chance that such a goal will be less than maximally challenging, but this may be more than offset by its ready acceptance. Previous performance is easily calculated where there are company records; but care must be taken to insure that the previous conditions of work were the same, or else adjustments will be necessary in order to take account of new circumstances.

For example, a forest products company developed mathematical equations to indicate how much wood could be cut as a function of the number and types of pieces of equipment, the size of the trees, and the spacing between the trees. Using statistical tables, which were compiled from previous experience, an expected level of production could be set for each new location. This expected level was then used as a goal for each logging crew.[6]

Sometimes the present job situation is unique or so new that there are no previous performance data that can be used to set goals. In such cases, goal setting becomes a matter of *judgment* based on the best knowledge available. As a manager, the judgment involved may be your own, in which case you would simply assign the goal to a subordinate. Or you may combine your judgment with that of one or more subordinates in cases where they have knowledge relevant to the task. This procedure is known as *participative goal setting*. If subordinates are especially competent and trustworthy, the goal setting process may be *delegated* to them.

When an organization has a formal management by objectives system, the managers' goals are designed to be congruent with the *organization's objectives*. The organization's objectives may be based, in part, on past organizational performance or, more importantly, on where the organization wants to go in the future, regardless of past achievements. An organization might, for example, decide to enter a new line of business, in which case there would be no past performance to form a basis for setting goals. Such goals must be based on judgment.

The MBO process involves *cascading* objectives. Goals are set first for the organization as a whole, perhaps by the Board of Directors. Then the top executives set goals that are congruent with the organization's goals. Each executive, in turn, meets with his or her subordinate managers, and together they set objectives that will help the executives reach their goals. Similarly, the managers meet with the supervisors who report to them. This process is carried all the way down to the lowest managerial level.[7]

While the MBO process is usually considered to be for

managers only, we believe that it can and should be extended to nonsupervisory personnel as well.[8] The goals set at each level help in achieving the goals at the next highest level. The goals of all employees combined are a means to achieving the organization's overall objectives.

A final consideration that can affect the goals that are set is the *external environment.* External pressures sometimes compel an organization to set certain objectives if it is to survive and remain competitive. For example, if a company is making hand calculators that sell for $14.95, and a competitor comes out with an equally good one selling for $9.95, the organization may have to cut prices (and hopefully costs) or see its market share significantly eroded. Other goals may be mandated by government regulations, for example, laws regarding pollution control, hiring, safety, and so forth.

4. Specify the time span involved. This involves setting a deadline for reaching the goal, for example, to answer each customer inquiry within ninety minutes.[9] For repetitive manual work, it is common to set goals for each day, for instance, to cut X number of trees today.

As the level of responsibility increases, it may become appropriate to increase the time span across which goals are projected. Thus, while semiskilled and blue collar workers may have daily or weekly goals, the goals of executives may be expressed in terms of months or years. Many American organizations seem to emphasize annual goals. However, some business people believe that this is too short a time span for effective strategic planning. They believe that organizations should be thinking in terms of three- to five-year goals so that long-term benefits will not be sacrificed for short-term results. It has been argued that such long-range planning is characteristic of successful Japanese companies.

5. Prioritize goals. As jobs increase in complexity, the number of different goals is also likely to increase. When more than one goal is set it becomes important to rank the goals in terms of their relative importance. The purpose of this step is to direct action and effort in proportion to the importance of each goal.

It is critical here that a consensus exist regarding goal priorities, so that each person knows exactly what is expected. It can be unfortunate, and even tragic, to give an employee a poor performance evaluation when the problem was not lack of competence but rather lack of knowledge as to what was expected.

To cite one example, an executive was hired by a national association to edit a series of publications. In an emergency, she was asked to take charge of the annual convention, and she spent a great deal of time planning the convention at the expense of her editorial work. After the convention, she was fired for not doing the editing job for which she had been hired! She had incorrectly prioritized her goals. If she had sought consensus on her priorities, her dismissal might not have occurred.

In a more successful example, consider Scott Paper's plant in Everett, Washington. The goals of the then plant manager and now vice president, Thomas Czepiel, were threefold. These were stated cogently and succinctly: (1) 511, (2) base business, and (3) all other. The number "511" referred to an innovative way of making an extremely high quality paper towel—Job Squad. The words "base business" referred to the profitability of the paper mill. "All other" referred to a miscellaneous category. "If what you are doing doesn't directly impact 511 or our base business, it is a low priority item," said Czepiel. Czepiel has the ability to crystallize the direction that he and his people will take. In setting these objectives, the wall that had gone up between the people in the start-up operation, 511, and the people in the base business came down and arguments over who should get what resource in terms of people and equipment ended. The plant was unified by stressing these three goals, with top priority being given to making 511 a success from an operating standpoint.

6. *Optional step: rate goals as to difficulty and importance.* If a high degree of quantification is desired in the case where multiple goals are set, each goal can be rated as to its difficulty and

importance. These ratings can be combined with a rating of degree of goal fulfillment in order to calculate an overall performance score for each individual. Consider, for example, the following numbers showing hypothetical scores for one manager:

GOAL	IMPORTANCE[a] $\times$	DEGREE OF GOAL DIFFICULTY[a] $\times$	DEGREE OF GOAL FULFILLMENT	= PRODUCT
A	10	8	.90	72.00
B	7	5	1.00	35.00
C	4	10	.50	20.00
D	1	6	.80	4.80
			Total Performance Score	131.80

[a]On a ten point scale (10 = most important or difficult).

The total score, obtained by summing the products, can be used on a comparative basis by ranking the scores of different individuals. To obtain an absolute score, the total score can be divided by the highest possible score. This can be calculated by entering all 1.00s in the "degree of goal fulfillment" column and recomputing the products. Thus in the above example the highest possible score is 80 + 35 + 40 + 6 = 161. On an absolute scale, this employee achieved 131.8 out of 161 possible points or 82 percent of maximum. Such percentage scores could conceivably be compared across different jobs, although caution should be used since many different judgments are involved in determining each total (that is, importance, difficulty, and degree of goal fulfillment must all be measured by judgment).

The advantage of the procedure shown above is that individuals are given credit for *trying for difficult goals even if they do not fully achieve them,* since their score depends on the degree of attainment as well as goal difficulty. Thus an employee who sets very easy goals and exceeds them might get a lower total score than one who sets hard goals and partially attains them. Similarly, an employee who reaches only low-priority goals and neglects those with high priorities could get lower scores than one who tries for the important goals and only partially achieves them.

Such considerations could scuttle the Senior Executive Service bonus system inaugurated by President Carter in the 1978 Civil Service Reform Act. Typically, government employees under this system are rewarded based on degree of goal attainment *regardless of the importance or difficulty of the goals involved.* Thus, an individual who sets and exceeds very easy goals for trivial aspects of the job could be rewarded at the expense of those who set more challenging goals for more important aspects of the job. This would negate the purpose of the whole system, which was designed to promote good performance.

7. Determine coordination requirements. Before settling on a final set of goals, it is important to determine whether achieving this set of goals is dependent on the cooperation and contribution of other individuals.[10] If so, it may be necessary to coordinate the goals of various individuals and to ensure that the goals of different people are not conflicting. Vertical coordination may be relatively easy with an MBO system, for example, since each manager will be aware of the goals of each subordinate. Conflicts are more likely to occur laterally[11]; thus there is a need for lateral integrating mechanisms.

When Peter Belluschi became, at the age of 37, an operations vice president of his own division for Weyerhaeuser Company, he realized that the responsibility for his firm's productivity could not be delegated to a productivity guru or czar. Productivity needed to be treated as a strategic issue.

Traditionally, productivity had been treated as a manufacturing problem, something to be dealt with by individual managers. But Belluschi felt that the real gains could be made by integrating the goals among departments as well as across units within a department. He felt that while the productivity of each individual business in his division could be improved, the greatest improvement in the division's productivity would come when problems among areas were addressed and resolved.

Belluschi himself did not know enough about the day-to-day operations of each of the major divisions of his region (pulp, timber, raw materials, wood products) to identify productivity improvement opportunities. Nor did he need or want to know—that was the job of his managers, superintendents, and foremen. Belluschi restricted his role, initially, to that of a sponsor, issuing two preliminary guidelines: (1) each of the four businesses was to set specific goals, including statements of the purpose of the business and its primary responsibilities; and (2) each business was to specify actual strategies for attaining the goals.

On completion of these two steps, Belluschi got together with his four business managers as a group. Together they analyzed the goals, the strategies, the likelihood of the success of these strategies, the consistency of an individual business's goals and strategies against the overall division's objectives, the risks involved, and the resources that would be required. Most importantly, however, they concentrated on how the strategies proposed by the various units would interact with each other. This led to decisions regarding the reorganization of the businesses in a new way. All of these decisions were the sort that only top management as a group can make.

The immediate benefit of this approach was that for the first time each business knew how it should interact with the other. Conflicts regarding "turf" were eliminated. Abdication of responsibility by one or more businesses, in the belief that the other business would assume it, ceased. Duplication—even triplication—of efforts stopped. A streamlining and an economy of effort occurred.

GROUP OR INDIVIDUAL GOALS?

The late Rensis Likert, a psychologist at the University of Michigan, argued that group goal setting fosters a higher degree of cooperation and communication than individual goal setting, and thus is preferable.[12] When the tasks to be accomplished are highly interdependent, group goals are indeed appropriate. But this is unlikely to be the case where the jobs are not interdependent.

Furthermore, certain cautions need to be noted concerning group goals. Bibb Latané, a psychologist at the University of North Carolina, has found that when individuals work in groups a phenomenon called *social loafing* often occurs.[13] Social loafing refers to the fact that the individuals put forth less effort when working in a group than when working alone on the same task, even though they believe that they are trying their hardest in both cases. Members of work groups seem to adopt an implicit premise that amounts to "Let Pat do it." Latané found that the key to social loafing is the belief that in a group the individual's contribution to the task cannot or will not be measured. When the individual's contribution to the group effort is measured, the social loafing phenomenon disappears.[14]

This has clear implications for the use of group goals: when group goals are set, specific provisions should be made for measuring the contributions of each member to the group product, and the members should be told that this is being done. Such measurements can be accomplished with the use of Behavioral Observation Scales, which were described earlier in this chapter. Such scales should be filled out by each group member on every other member. In addition to motivating high performance, such measurements would provide a basis for giving individual performance appraisals as well as promoting future employee development. Learning theory in psychology as well as various theories of motivation emphasize that feedback must occur at the level of the individual if successful appraisal and development is to take place.

The optimal strategy, of course, is to set goals for the group as well as for each individual within the group. This is often what occurs in effective teambuilding and quality circle sessions. The groups decide on a common objective, and action steps (goals) are then set showing who will do what, when.

GOAL MODIFICATION

Goals are typically based on knowledge of the past and certain predictions regarding the future. Since no one is omniscient, such predictions will sometimes be wrong, and new conditions may require modification of previously set goals if the new situation makes them inappropriate. However, goals should not be changed frivolously every time an obstacle arises. After all, the purpose of goal setting is to motivate employees to overcome or remove obstacles in order to reach their goals.

A key role of a supervisor is to identify such obstacles and to work with a subordinate to find ways of overcoming them. Furthermore, if goals are treated as guidelines for enhancing performance and developing employees rather than as weapons to punish nonperformers, it is no great tragedy if a given goal is not reached. The employee can still try to get as close as possible to the goal.

Nothing breeds success like success. Conversely, nothing causes feelings of despair like perpetual failure. A primary purpose of goal setting is to increase the motivation level of the individual. But goal setting can have precisely the opposite effect if it produces a yardstick that constantly makes the individual feel inadequate. Consequently, the supervisor must be on the lookout for unrealistic goals and be prepared to change them when necessary. If goals turn out to be unrealistic because employees lack the skills needed to attain them, the goals may be lowered while the employees gain more experience or undergo additional training. For example, one clerical supervisor who set goals for each clerk observed that two clerks (due to lack of experience) were unable to attain their goals. Their goals were immediately lowered until the clerks acquired enough skill to attain them. Later, their goals were raised to the level of the more experienced employees.

It should be noted that, in the previous example, the organization did not punish anyone for failing to reach her goal. Nor, in this case, was any specific, tangible reward offered for goal attainment. Thus employees did not rebel or lash out at their supervisors or become depressed when they initially failed to attain their goals or when their goals were later increased. Goal setting was used here only as a guide, as an incentive to performance, and as a means of promoting pride in accomplishment.[15]

Assuming employees have sufficient knowledge to perform their tasks adequately, goal modification is advisable only when conditions have changed so drastically that the goal difficulty level is grossly inappropriate or the content of the goals themselves is irrelevant. For example, if halfway through the year an organization is faced with a severe financial crisis, the goal to increase market share might be abandoned in favor of the goal to increase immediate cash flow.

SUMMARY

The seven key steps in goal setting are as follows:

1. Specify the nature of the task(s) to be accomplished (that is, write a job description). This may be done in terms of work outcomes and/or in terms of work actions or behaviors.

2. Specify how performance is to be measured.

3. Specify the standard or target to be aimed for in quantitative terms based either on directly measured output or on a Behavioral Observation Scale. Make the goal challenging, that is, difficult but attainable.

4. Specify the time span involved.

5. If there are multiple goals, rank them in terms of importance or priority. Get a consensus on this ranking.

6. If necessary, rate each goal quantitatively as to importance (priority) and difficulty. To measure overall performance, multiply importance by difficulty by degree of goal attainment, and then sum the products.

7. Determine the coordination requirements (especially lateral) for goal achievement. If the tasks are highly interdependent, use group goals. If group goals are used, be sure to develop a means of measuring each individual's contribution to the group's product. The goals should be modified only if employees clearly lack the ability or knowledge needed to reach them or when substantial changes in the job situation have occurred.

5 • *Obtaining goal commitment*

In this chapter we discuss the *sine qua non* of goal setting, namely, obtaining goal commitment. Unless the individual and/or work group is committed to goal attainment, the setting of specific, hard goals obviously will have no effect on job performance.

There are at least six methods that can be used alone or in combination to obtain employee commitment to performance goals. These methods are instruction and explanation, supervisory supportiveness, employee participation in the goal setting process, training to ensure sufficient knowledge, valid selection procedures to ensure employee capability, and the use of incentives and rewards.

INSTRUCTION AND EXPLANATION

Explaining goals and the reasons behind them are often sufficient to gain employee commitment to goals provided that the boss's demands are considered legitimate. Simple instructions that included an explanation and an absence of threats or intimidation were enough to ensure goal acceptance in most of our studies. The key here is for subordinates to perceive a goal as fair and reasonable. Furthermore, they must trust management; if they perceive a goal as exploitative, they are likely to reject it.

41

In the experiment with woods workers described in Chapter 2, the problem of obtaining goal commitment was potentially difficult.[1] The logging supervisors, being independent businessmen who supplied timber to the Georgia Kraft Company, were not required to follow Georgia Kraft's advice regarding how to motivate employees. The company, however, was interested in loggers' ability to provide a continuous supply of its primary raw material—wood. Consequently, under the auspices of the American Pulpwood Association it sponsored the following goal setting experiment.

Seven company employees, who were aware of the aims and objectives of the logger's job, who frequently observed these particular logging crews on the job site, and who were well known by the logging crews, were given instructions on the value and techniques of goal setting. A three-hour program was conducted in which the purpose of this experiment and the assumptions underlying it were explained.

Each forester then contacted the selected loggers and requested their participation in the study. The loggers were told that the purpose of this study was to give them a one-day training program on how to set specific production goals and how to determine the subsequent effects of using goals on performance. The potential value of goal setting was discussed for an hour, and the remainder of the day was spent showing the loggers how to use production tables for setting goals. One of the training handouts given to both the logging experts employed by Georgia Kraft and the independent logging businessmen is shown in Table 3.

For four major reasons, the concept of goal setting was readily accepted by the loggers and their crews. First, the explanation of the value of goal setting stressed that setting specific goals would help each logger to increase productivity without additional capital outlays. Second, the program was voluntary; the people could drop out of the progam at any time, so there was no reason to feel threatened by it. Third, the production tables, which showed expected production based on the past performance of crews working under similar conditions, made

Table 3 • American Pulpwood Association—Harvesting Research Project

February 15, 1971

TO: Georgia Kraft foresters and pulpwood dealers participating in the APA Harvesting Research Project's training program on the motivational effects of goal setting.

SUBJECT: Explanation of study to participating pulpwood producers in the experimental (training) group.

Gentlemen:

The following comments should assist you in explaining the purpose of this research program to pulpwood producers and their employees.

Since 1968 Georgia Kraft and five Southern paper companies have contributed over two million dollars to the American Pulpwood Association—Harvesting Research Project to find new and easier ways of increasing pulpwood production. Because they recognize that without people like you the entire paper industry could not exist, they have focused their attention on methods that you can use to increase your profits.

In the past, our recommendations have often been limited to suggestions that you purchase a piece of equipment that costs $16,000 or more. Although you may have agreed that it would be great to own that equipment, you were hesitant about making such a heavy economic investment. As a result Georgia Kraft and the Harvesting Research Project searched for a method that would result in a substantial increase in your income.

Four studies by the Harvesting Research Project and the Georgia Kraft 1970 annual producer survey involving over one thousand producers have yielded very encouraging results. We have found that if you stay on the job with your men and set a weekly production goal you can increase your productivity and reduce your injuries at no extra financial cost to you or your employees.

We would like to set up a training program in which we will teach you and your men to set systematic production goals that take into account the type of terrain on which you are working. This program is used by all of Georgia Kraft's company crews and has resulted in a substantial increase in profits for the company. You are under no obligation, however, to Georgia Kraft or the American Pulpwood Association—Harvesting Research Project if you participate in this study; you may quit this study at any time. The entire cost of the program is paid for by the Harvesting Research Project. All that we ask is that you promise not to tell anyone about the study until we are completed. This secrecy is necessary because you are one of 36 people in the entire United States who will receive this information. Before we can release the news to everyone, we need evidence that our training program will work for independent producers at no cost to themselves.

The training itself will only take one day. We will then ask you each week for 14 weeks such simple questions as, how many cords of wood did you produce, how many men were injured, did anyone quit their job?

The entire procedure is very easy. All you have to do is:

1. Determine the average diameter breast height (dbh) of the stand being harvested on the tract. Simply measure or estimate the dbh of 30 or 40 trees to the nearest inch and take the dbh which occurs the most often as being the average.
2. Enter the table given you for your operation with this diameter and read off the number for a given day.
3. This represents the number of trees which each sawhand should produce in a 8 or 9 hour day. You will note the cords are also given in the same table.
4. Give each sawhand his goal for the day and/or week.
5. The sawhand tallies each processed tree on the tally meter supplied by company personnel.

If there are any questions concerning this procedure, do not hesitate to ask the company representative assisting you with the study. Also, any comments concerning the method or ways for improvement should be forwarded to the company.

SOURCE: Reprinted with permission of the American Pulpwood Association.

it clear to the crews that the goals were not capricious but rather were based on objective data. Fourth, the crews were paid on a piece-rate basis, so any increases in productivity benefited them directly.

One gratifying—and very important—result of this study was that despite the increase in production achieved, goal setting did not increase either turnover or injuries. The company's initial fear was that goal setting might speed up production to the point that people would become careless and get hurt, or become sufficiently upset that they would quit. The actual results demonstrate that a logical explanation of the value of goal setting combined with "how-to-do-it" instructions may be sufficient, even when the goal setters are not directly employed by those who initiate the program.

Of course, the independent loggers were paid on a piece-rate basis; but while monetary rewards can play a role in ensuring goal commitment (as we shall discuss in a later chapter), their role is not indispensable. The Georgia Kraft Company replicated the previous study with its own logging crews, who were paid by the hour rather than by the piece. The results from simple instructions on the value of goal setting were dramatic. The increases in production per payroll hour for each of the six crews were 3 percent, 10 percent, 13 percent, 41 percent, 44 percent, and 116 percent (mean = 37.8 percent). This resulted in an overall cost savings of $2.63 per cord as compared to the previous year. After twelve months the increases in production were 10.3 percent, 50.0 percent, 18.4 percent, 34.8 percent, 35.7 percent, and 56.4 percent (mean = 34.3 percent) for the same crews.

In this study, the fact that the request to set and meet goals was made directly by the employer (i.e., that it presumably was perceived as a legitimate exercise of managerial authority) undoubtedly facilitated goal acceptance. However, it should be stressed that in no case was anyone punished or chastised for failing to attain a goal. Supervisors took a supportive rather than a punitive attitude and this helped the goal setting program to succeed.

SUPERVISORY SUPPORTIVENESS

The role of supportive relationships is a key part of modern theories of organizational leadership. Rensis Likert, the late director of the Institute of Social Research at the University of Michigan, concluded from years of field research that to be effective, leaders must adhere to the principle of supportive relationships.[2] In essence, this principle states that a leader should build and maintain each subordinate's sense of personal worth. Likert went on to argue that the more often a supervisor is supportive toward the subordinate, the greater will be the effect of the supervisor's behavior on the subordinate's performance.

To test this proposition, we conducted an experiment in the laboratory.[3] A laboratory setting was used because of the practical and ethical questions that would have been raised by a field experiment in manipulating supportiveness. In the supportive situation, the supervisor (1) gave the person a friendly welcome, (2) reassured the person that he or she would do well, (3) used words of encouragement and support (e.g., "Do you feel comfortable with that goal?"), (4) encouraged the person to ask questions, and (5) asked rather than told the person to do things.

In the nonsupportive situation, the supervisor (1) told the person that he was in a hurry, (2) told the person to listen closely because he did not have a lot of time, (3) tossed rather than handed the sheet of paper to the person, and (4) continually glanced at his watch. Generally, the supervisor behaved in a rude and abrupt manner.

Both the people whose boss was supportive and the people whose boss was nonsupportive accepted their goals. But the people whose boss behaved supportively set or accepted much higher goals than those whose boss was nonsupportive. Thus, the study showed that supportiveness on the part of supervisors is important because it gives people the confidence and trust to set or accept high goals, which in turn lead to high levels of performance.

EMPLOYEE PARTICIPATION

For the past thirty years organizational theorists have argued that employee participation in decision-making is the primary means of increasing employee commitment to productivity and lowering employee resistance to change. Such theorists would predict, for example, that employees who do not participate in the process of setting their goals would not accept them.

Surprisingly, research findings give very little support to this assumption.[4] Studies on performance improvement done at General Electric [5], for example, showed that *how* a goal is set (participatively or nonparticipatively) is not as important as that a specific goal *is* set.

To check on the reliability of this one finding, which contradicted the thinking of so many other organizational scholars, we conducted eleven additional studies on participation in goal setting, some in the laboratory and some in field settings.[6] The people studied included loggers, typists, engineers, scientists, supervisors, and college students. With one exception, the results were remarkably consistent: letting employees participate in the process of setting goals led to no greater goal commitment and no higher productivity than did assigning them goals. Participation affects performance only when it leads to the setting of goals that are higher than is the case when the supervisor assigns them unilaterally. When goal difficulty is the same, there is no difference in the performance of those with assigned versus participatively set goals. The exception to this conclusion occurred in a brainstorming session where those people in the participative goal setting group understood their task better than did the people who were simply assigned goals. In the process of participating in the setting of goals, these people took the time to ask questions regarding expectations of them.

Our finding that participation in goal setting does not consistently lead to higher productivity than simply assigning goals agrees with a recent review of early studies on participation in decision-making.[7] Participation in decision-making should be regarded as a pragmatic rather than a moral issue. And even the pragmatic issue is often clouded by the acceptance of a false dichotomy, namely, that management must use either an authoritarian approach or a participative one.

The practice of assigning goals does not have to be and should not be authoritarian, with all of its perjorative concomitants (e.g., cold, arbitrary, threatening, demanding of obedience for the sake of obedience). Goals should be assigned in a supportive atmosphere, and they should be based on logical reasoning. On the other hand, our research does not indicate that participation in goal setting is harmful, but only that it may not be necessary in many cases. Thus managers are certainly justified in using it, if and when they think it advisable. Moreover, it is important to note that participation, while not usually necessary in *setting* goals, may be very useful when it comes to *implementing* them.[8] Here we are more concerned with the generation of ideas—for example, creative and useful techniques for attaining goals. In this respect, there is a parallel to quality circles. Quality circles are not designed to allow employees to set quality goals but to find ways to achieve them, that is, to improve product quality.

The potential effectiveness of employee participation as a means of generating ideas is shown by the results achieved at the A. E. Staley Manufacturing Company plant in Lafayette, Indiana.[9] Employees there work in teams of ten to fourteen people. The employees are treated as "self-managers" in that they decide, as a team, how their work is to be done as long as they attain their production goals. Management retains only a few prerogatives, controlling the pay scale, emphasizing safety, and assigning production goals to employees. The rest is left up to the work force. This includes deciding who is hired, who is fired, who gets a raise, who works when, and who needs disciplining for not doing his or her share. In short, management sets the goals; employees participate in the decisions as to who will do what, when, and where in order to attain them.

Since it opened in 1977, the $120 million plant has been expanded twice, in part because demand for the company's product, corn syrup, has grown, and in part because the employees keep exceeding the production goals assigned to them, thus keeping costs down. In addition turnover is one-half of 1 percent compared to over 20 percent in a sister plant, where employee participation is not practiced; and absenteeism is 1.4 percent versus 3 to 4 percent in the sister plant.

So, do not conclude that we are recommending the assignment of goals to employees as a superior alternative to employee participation. What we are saying is that participation is not essential for goal acceptance. As A. E. Staley noted, "The key is building trust." Participation may or may not be needed to achieve it.

TRAINING

Some employees may resist the goal setting process because they feel they lack the ability and knowledge to attain their goals. Motivation without knowledge is useless, so selection and training are essential. The supervisor must know the capabilities of the subordinates to whom goals are assigned. Asking an employee to formulate an action plan for reaching the goal, as in management by objectives (MBO), can be very useful, as it may reveal areas of ignorance.

A comprehensive review of the training literature is beyond the scope of this book.[10] However, it should be noted that it is not only the employee who may be in need of training on how to attain goals in order for goal setting to be effective; it may very well be the supervisor who needs training in how to set them.

For example, a division of a large national manufacturer and distributor of office equipment supplies and electronic systems recently evaluated the effectiveness of two training programs.[11] The purpose of the training programs, directed by Dr. John Ivancevich of the University of Houston, was to make sales managers more effective in assigning goals to sales representatives (reps) than they had been during the three years in which the goal setting program had been in effect.

Prior to the training, no formal instruction in goal setting procedures had been provided to the managers. The firm had relied on a standard operating manual that described the process, the sequence, and the forms used. A copy of the manual had been given to each manager. The managers were expected to learn how to assign goals and counsel the reps on goal setting matters.

The sales managers were randomly assigned to one of three groups: a group trained through the use of modeling, role playing, and videotaped feedback; a group trained via a lecture and role playing; or a control group. In the first group, the trainees were given a one-hour lecture on goal setting procedures, followed by three videotapes (models) of appropriate goal setting skills and styles. The trainees were then divided into two-person groups for role playing. Pairs of trainees acted out the roles of superior and subordinate using two instructional scripts. Both trainers and peers provided feedback on each role playing experience.

After the exercise, each member critiqued a videotape of his or her own performance that had been recorded prior to the lecture, watching the models, and role playing the desired behaviors. Their original performance was also critiqued at this time by another group. The entire training period lasted approximately three and one-half hours.

In the second group, the trainees received the same one-hour lecture on goal setting, and then they role-played as superior and subordinate. Both trainers and peers provided feedback on each role play performance.

The results showed the two groups did not differ significantly from one another. However, both groups scored significantly better than the no training group on such variables as production (orders/sales presentations; new accounts) and reps' perceptions of supportiveness, challenge, clarity, feedback, and job satisfaction.

It may be inferred from this finding that employees are more likely to accept goals set by trained managers than by untrained managers. Furthermore, the training program may have increased the manager's own acceptance of goal setting as an effective tool.

SELECTION PROCEDURES

The flip-side of the coin of training people to set and/or attain goals is to select people with the ability to perform the job or the capability of acquiring the needed skills.

The concept of goal setting can be used in conducting selection interviews. The underlying assumption is that a person's goals, intentions, and plans are related to subsequent behavior. If what people say in an interview correlates highly with what they do later on the job, the advantage of using the interview for making selection decisions is obvious. The interview would approximate a sample of actual job behaviors, and the need for expensive aptitude tests or job simulation procedures would be reduced.

A potential problem with the interview, one that is generally not a weakness of aptitude tests or job simulations, is faking. Many interviewees can quickly discern from the wording of a question what answer the interviewer wants to hear. A procedure that overcomes this problem and predicts performance on the job is the *situational interview*.[12] It is effective because it identifies the persons's intentions. Four steps are followed:

First, a job analysis is conducted to provide a comprehensive (content-valid) description of the critical knowledge, skills, and behaviors that a person must demonstrate on the job. The job analysis procedure used in the situational interview is the *critical incident technique,* or CIT.[13] In using the CIT, job experts are asked to recall incidents that they themselves have observed during the past six to twelve months that proved especially effective or ineffective in accomplishing one or more aspects of the job.

Second, the experts choose one or two incidents that best exemplify the job aspect or criterion of interest. For example, superintendents of a sawmill identified nine key areas in which a foreman must be competent. These areas include safety, interaction with peers, and work habits.

Third, the incidents are used to construct questions. Literary license is taken in turning the incident into a situation where the answer is not obvious to the listener, but the situation is nevertheless one that the applicant is likely to encounter on the job.

An example of a critical incident describing the ineffective behavior of an hourly employee is:

> The employee was devoted to his family. He had been married for only 18 months. He used whatever excuse he could to stay home. One day the fellow's baby got a cold. His wife had a hangnail or something on her toe. He didn't come to work. He didn't even phone in.

This incident was rewritten by supervisors in the form of the following question:

> Your spouse and two teenage children are sick in bed with colds. There are no relatives or friends available to look in on them. Your shift starts in three hours. What would you do in this situation?

Fourth, a scoring guide is developed. This step is important because interviewers are often unable to agree among themselves as to the appropriateness of the answers they hear. Thus, it is little wonder that it has been shown repeatedly across industries that the interview, as typically used, is generally a poor tool for selection purposes. The scoring guide uses benchmark answers to assist the interviewer(s) score an answer on a scale of 1 to 5. The three benchmarks for the above question were:

> 1. I'd stay home—my spouse and family come first. (Poor answer)
> 3. I'd phone my supervisor and explain my situation. (Acceptable answer)
> 5. Since they only have colds, I'd come to work. (Excellent answer)

This approach to interviewing has been shown to be effective in selecting hourly as well as supervisory employees, blacks as well as whites, and males as well as females. By selecting competent, motivated employees, acceptance and achievement of specific challenging goals on the job is more likely to occur than when these types of people are not hired.

INCENTIVES AND REWARDS

An obvious reason why goals may be rejected is that the employee sees no personal benefit, either in terms of personal pride or in terms of external rewards like money or promotion, in working to attain them. Even worse, the employee may perceive the consequences of goal attainment to be aversive (e.g., she may encounter peer ridicule).

Obviously, one positive incentive for accepting and attaining goals is money. However, the use of monetary incentives is so complex that we have saved our discussion of it for another chapter. But in addition to money, there are a number of other incentives that can promote goal acceptance.

One of them is to *please the boss*. Since most people want to get along with their superiors, they are unlikely to provoke a confrontation over the issue of accepting assigned goals, especially if they consider the goals to be legitimate and reasonable.

Another incentive for goal acceptance is *the anticipation that goals will make the job fun*. As we noted earlier, many jobs are boring and repetitive. Most employees welcome the chance to experience challenge and excitement in their work—to provide themselves a sense of purpose. When they reach a goal, there is usually a feeling of pride in performance. This occurs even in plants with less than cordial union–management relations; provided that the unions are convinced that goals will not be used punitively, they typically do not object to them. (See Chapter 10 for details.)

The supervisor or manager can make goal attainment more appealing by *giving recognition* for it. Recognition can take many forms, such as a thank you, a congratulatory statement, a note in the person's personnel file, an announcement at a company function, a name posted on the bulletin board (e.g., employee of the month), a prize, a letter, and so on. Recognition, of course, necessarily involves *feedback*.

At IBM, employees are systematically prodded toward excellence by providing them with very specific goals. Achievement is immediately followed by rewards. Insiders say that the most cherished reward is not money:

> It's having your name and quota on the bulletin board with a notation saying "100%." It's having a party thrown for you at your branch because you satisfied a prickly customer. It's a steady flow of letters of commendation. The notes and the quotes, the praise and the parties are very effective: people work their brains out.[14]

The hard work, resulting from IBM's emphasis on hard goals, inspires another effect. A clique forms from the pressure everyone feels; the first thing employees want to do at night is go out and have a drink together. Then they start blending business and social life, and a desire to learn from one another is enhanced.

When performance is measured and fed back to employees in a quantitative form, it is common for *informal competition* to arise spontaneously among them. Most employees like to "beat the other person." Competition injects an element of excitement and challenge into the job and promotes pride in accomplishment. For example, as a result of goal setting, unionized truck drivers began to record their truck weight in a pocket notebook, and they found themselves bragging about their accomplishments to their co-workers.[15] They also viewed goal setting as a challenge. For a more dramatic example, consider the following story told by steel titan Charles M. Schwab. One of his plant managers was achieving below average production:

> "How is it that a man as able as you," I asked him one day, "cannot make this mill turn out what it should?"
> "I don't know," he replied; "I have coaxed the men; I have pushed them; I have sworn at them. I have done everything in my power. Yet they will not produce."
> It was near the end of the day; in a few minutes the

night force would come on duty. I turned to a workman who was standing beside one of the red-mouthed furnaces and asked him for a piece of chalk.

"How many heats has your shift made today?" I queried.

"Six," he replied.

I chalked a big "6" on the floor, and then passed along without another word. When the night shift came in they saw the "6" and asked about it.

"The big boss was in here today," said the day men. "He asked us how many heats we had made, and we told him six. He chalked it down."

The next morning I passed through the same mill. I saw that the "6" had been rubbed out and a big "7" written instead. The night shift had announced itself. That night I went back. The "7" had been erased, and a "10" swaggered in its place. The day force recognized no superiors. Thus a fine competition was started, and it went on until this mill, formerly the poorest producer, was turning out more than any other mill in the plant.[16]

While we do not recommend encouraging too much formal competition (since it may lead to losers becoming apathetic and winners being more concerned with ways of winning rather than with what is best for the company), informal or spontaneous competition certainly fosters goal commitment.

Another way to encourage goal commitment is through *constructive social pressure,* as is often the case in teambuilding. Teambuilding occurs when a group of people whose work is interrelated agree to come together to (1) identify problems of mutual concern, (2) prioritize those problems, (3) brainstorm solutions, (4) agree on those solutions, and (5) set goals as to who will do what, by when. Typically, teambuilding meetings also determine whether employees have adequate resources—money, equipment, time, help, and freedom to utilize them—to attain goals, and whether company policies work to facilitate or block goal attainment.

Scott Paper Company uses teambuilding regularly among

its executives, managers, and foremen, and it has been especially effective in establishing a productive working relationship with the union. The teambuilding that occurs between company and the union is called *relations by objectives* (RBO). The purpose of RBO is to identify goals that the company and the union can work together to attain. The only agreed-on limit to RBO discussions is that the collective bargaining process not be circumvented. Thus, the emphasis is solely on how management and the union can work together effectively under the current management–labor contract. Peer pressures make for high goal commitment on the part of all who participate in the process.

Organizations must also be on the lookout for factors that work *against* goal commitment. A common source of resistance to high productivity when using piece-rate systems is *the fear that rates would be cut*, forcing employees to work harder just to get the same pay. This fear may often be justified since rate cutting does occur. Rate cutting, however, is becoming less common, because unions oppose such cuts and because employers are becoming aware of the futility of actions that breed distrust among the labor force.

Another longstanding source of resistance to goal setting is *fear of layoffs*. Very few employees will strive for high goals today if they suspect they are working themselves out of a job. Thus organizations need to do whatever they can to promote a reasonable degree of *job security* among their employees if they want them to enthusiastically pursue challenging production goals. Although absolute job security can rarely, if ever, be guaranteed, it helps to know that as a matter of policy the organization tries to minimize layoffs and engages in long-term manpower planning and work scheduling. A strategy adopted by several of our clients is to set specific hard production goals, share cost information with the union and the work force, talk frankly about commitments, and stress the tradeoff of "producing more at less labor cost," which in a down market will certainly result in curtailments, but will hopefully result in the long-term survival of the organization and the jobs that it supplies.

SUMMARY

Goal acceptance is a *sine qua non* of effective goal setting. In most cases goal acceptance can be assured simply by asking the employee to accept reasonable goals and giving an explanation of why such goals are beneficial to the employee and the company. Supportiveness on the part of the boss is also helpful; supervisors and managers must show real interest in their subordinates' concerns about goal setting and help them to formulate action plans that will result in goal attainment. Participation in setting goals is not usually necessary for obtaining goal acceptance. Participation, however, may be extremely useful for developing plans and techniques for implementing goals. Goal acceptance is also easier when managers are thoroughly trained in the principles of goal setting and when those pursuing the goals are trained in the appropriate skills. Proper selection of employees is also essential, and this can be done in part by the use of a situational interview organized around the principle of goal setting. Goal acceptance is also facilitated by incentives such as money (to be discussed later), pleasing the boss, anticipation or challenge of the job, pride in accomplishment, recognition for goal attainment, feedback, spontaneous competition, and constructive peer pressure. Steps must be taken to insure that there are no negative incentives for goal acceptance, such as losing one's job.

6 • *Implementing goal setting*

In this chapter we identify the various conditions within the organization that help to make goal setting work.

ACTION PLANS

Action plans describe the means to accomplishing objectives. The development of the action plan should entail a means–ends as well as a cost–benefit analysis of various alternative actions in order to achieve a specific goal.

The development of action plans differs in scope across organizational levels. Action plans can focus on the global, long-term, and complex strategic mission of the organization, or they can focus narrowly on the most immediate decisions for accomplishing the simplest tasks. Viewing the organization as a hierarchy of management functions will facilitate an understanding of the appropriate breadth and time span for the action plan for a specific level. The typical organization consists of a top level management group including the president, vice presidents, and other corporate officers; a middle and lower level management group consisting of division heads, department superintendents, and supervisors; and the lowest level including nonmanagerial workers. Table 4 illustrates the type of action plans that are typically associated with the three levels of management.

Table 4 • Action Plans by Management Levels

MANAGEMENT LEVEL	ACTION PLAN CHARACTERISTIC
Top management	Long time span, strategic
Middle and lower management	Medium time span, tactical
Nonmanagerial	Short time span, procedural

The action plans of top management are generally strategic and long-term in focus. Strategic plans provide an underlying and unifying basis for all other plans to be developed within the organization. The long-range strategic plan provides information about an organization's basic direction and purpose, thus serving as a guide for all the operational activities of the organization.[1] The strategic plan provides constraints over the tactical plans of lower management levels. The "means" or action plans at the upper level frequently become the basis for specific goals at lower organizational levels. That is, lower level goals are a means to accomplishing subsets of higher level goals. For example, consider the strategic plan adopted by General Motors in the early 1920s to compete with Ford Motor Company for a larger share of the automotive market. At that time, Ford was having great success with the Model T, an all-purpose car priced to appeal to the large, middle-class income group in America. In order to capture a larger share of the potential market, top management at General Motors came up with the strategy of developing several different lines of cars, thus appealing to consumers at all income levels. This strategy, developed at the highest levels of management, served to unify and focus the efforts of the entire company. The specification by top management of definite price ranges for each new model served to establish targets for each of the operating divisions. The division producing the lowest priced car had to stay within the range of $450 to $600. The operating division assigned to produce the highest priced car was required to stay within the range of $2,500 to $3,500.[2]

The action plans of middle and lower management, consistent with their lesser levels of specialization and responsibility, are more tactical in nature than the plans of top management. The time frame of concern is of medium duration. Action plans developed at the middle management level specify the means to attain various factors outlined in the strategic plans of top executives. For example, R. Atkins, a department manager for International Metals Corporation, was instructed by the company president to focus on maximizing profits after having successfully achieved the largest growth in sales volume of any trading department over the years. Atkins set for himself a goal of $200,000 in profits for the following year.

> This objective made him look critically at each of the commodities he was trading in terms of its contribution toward achieving it. He did this by comparing the gross margin of each potential trade with the direct expenses involved in making the trade, plus the general overhead which was allocated to his department. As a longstanding company policy, general overhead was allocated on the basis of the dollar sales generated by each trader. Atkins had broken down all of his costs to a per pound basis so he could quickly determine the break-even point and profitability of any transaction. He was constantly searching for new profitable commodities in which to trade to replace those whose profit margins had eroded.[3]

The jobs of nonmanagerial employees are typically specialized and less complex than those of employees in higher positions. Goal accomplishment, therefore, is frequently obtained in a less complex form of activity, e.g., paying closer attention, working faster. The action plan (or procedural focus) at such a level is nevertheless a useful device for developing better means of goal attainment. Developing the action plan may stimulate creativity even in routine jobs. As discussed earlier, truck drivers in a large wood products company were given a difficult but attainable goal in terms of the percentage truck net weight to be hauled on each run.[4] Besides focusing greater attention and effort on this area of responsibility, a number of drivers recommended minor modifications on their trucks to help increase the accuracy of their judgments of weight.

To develop an action plan, then, requires that the individual or group should carefully define the desired goal and then search for an effective, efficient means of accomplishing it. This search will reveal possible alternative means whose desirability and feasibility can be examined. The examination of means may show in turn that existing or previously used strategies, tactics, or procedures have served quite well in the accomplishment of a particular objective and should continue to be used. However, a new or innovative means of attaining a particular goal is often needed. The organization may lack the experience, technology, or talent necessary to implement a plan for goal attainment. The organization may need new ideas or methods to solve a particularly thorny problem or to uproot a traditional approach that has proved ineffective in producing results. In such cases the action plan can suggest alternative resources, in addition to those available within the company, that may facilitate goal attainment.

Outside experts, consultants, trade associations, customers, and/or equipment manufacturers can be valuable sources of new ideas and methods and can provide a much larger pool of talent, specialization, and expertise than may be available within the organization. What happens when top management experts question the utility of past practice? Consider the case of Anheuser-Busch, Inc.[5]

Each year the vice president of marketing for Anheuser-Busch would approach Mr. Busch, the President and Chairman of the Board, with a proposal for $1,200,000 in advertising funds over budget based on the belief that such funds would help the firm increase sales. Busch always accepted this annual proposal and, in the year in question, was prepared to approve it once again. However, this time he began to wonder just how cost-effective this traditional practice was, so he called in outside experts to analyze ad expenditures.

The consultants proposed an experiment to test the effectiveness of additional advertising in increasing sales. Busch accepted their proposal of using only half of the requested funds in six of the twelve marketing areas originally targeted by the vice president. The consultants planned to measure how actual monthly sales deviated from forecasted sales for each marketing area. Six areas would receive the additional advertising, and six areas would not; thus an experimental group and a control group were created. After six months, results showed no difference in sales between the two groups. But the study did not stop here.

Busch's next question was how to determine what amount *should* be spent on advertising and how advertising effectiveness could be improved. Working with the marketing department and the contracted advertising agency, the consultants conducted a series of experimental studies to address these questions. Over a period of several years, their findings significantly improved the effectiveness and efficiency of the firm's advertising.

It is important to note in this example that Busch did not initially perceive the situation as a problem to overcome but rather was interested in examining the effectiveness of an often-used action plan. This type of questioning is one of the fundamental advantages of a cost–benefit analysis approach to action planning.

Carroll and Tosi summarized the reasons why action plans help organizations attain goals or objectives at all levels[6]:

1. Action plans aid in the search for more efficient methods of accomplishing objectives.
2. They provide an opportunity to test whether the objectives as stated can be accomplished.
3. They develop a sound basis for estimating time and/or cost requirements, and deadlines for accomplishment of goals.
4. They create an opportunity to examine the degree to which one will have to rely on other people in the organization for coordination and support.
5. They uncover unanticipated snags or barriers to accomplishment.

6. They determine the resources (personnel, equipment, supplies, facilities) required to accomplish the objectives.

7. They facilitate control of performance if the task is well-specified and agreed on; reporting need only occur when problems arise in implementation. This is a form of planning ahead; when plans are sufficiently complete, only deviations from them need to be communicated.

8. They identify areas in which the supervisor can provide support or assistance.

9. They facilitate the process of delegating authority.

FEEDBACK

A second condition that can significantly affect goal attainment is knowledge of results, or *feedback*, regarding performance. As noted in previous chapters, feedback is necessary in order to track progress toward desired outcomes. When people are given information on how well they are doing in relation to some expected standard, they can modify their behavior, if necessary, or continue their present course if it is shown to be effective.

There are two basic kinds of feedback: *cueing* and *summary feedback*. The first tells people how they are performing at the time they are actually taking action. Cues are often necessary even on familar tasks. For example, a major league pitcher would have serious trouble achieving or even maintaining any kind of accuracy in his pitching if he were prevented from knowing where the ball went after leaving his hand. Cueing often occurs when an individual monitors his or her own actions. It can be supplemented by tapes, films, and feedback from others.

Summary feedback tells a person his or her total performance to date on a task. It is greatly facilitated by the use of *feedback charts*. Such charts may also include a specification of the goal or target level for that job, so that differences between expected and actual performance stand out visually on the page.

While individual workers can keep their own charts, the supervisor may wish to construct charts showing the progress of the group, as well as that of each individual. A sample chart used by a forest products company is shown in Chapter 10 (Figure 5).

Another example is provided by an experiment conducted at Parkdale Mills, Inc., which was designed to improve declining attendance. The employees agreed to set as their goal an average level of 93 percent attendance for three weeks. A daily attendance chart was posted in the work area. Every employee's name was entered on the chart; a blue dot was placed on the chart for each day that the employee was present and a red dot for each day that the employee was absent. A weekly attendance graph was also posted in the work area to indicate the percent of employees who were present each day. The goal of 93 percent was indicated on the graph with a horizontal colored line.

Each person who came to work was complimented by the shift supervisor each day. When a person was absent, he or she was welcomed back the next day. No reprimand was given. Instead, the supervisor showed the employee the attendance chart, which was updated daily, and asked for help in getting the department to reach its goal of 93 percent.

From the baseline average of 86 percent, attendance increased immediately after the implementation of the program procedures (see Figure 4). For the following nine-week period, attendance averaged 94.3 percent. It was 100 percent one week, a record never before attained. Equally important, the supervisor reported that during this nine-week period the enthusiasm and teamwork that previously were lacking among these people improved greatly. The employees expressed pride in their accomplishment, and verbalized their commitment to continue this level of performance.

The costs of this program were less than ten dollars for the graph paper and the dots needed for the chart. Parkdale Mills, Inc., estimates that this program saved thirty dollars per day resulting in an annual savings of approximately $9,000. Additional savings were realized in terms of operating efficiency and

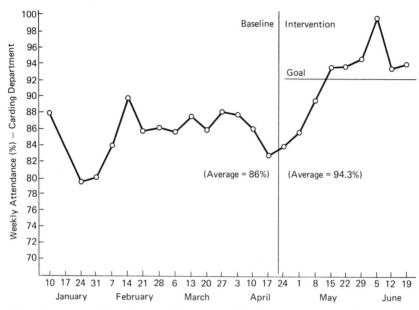

From Lawrence Miller, *Behavior Management: The New Science of Managing People at Work* (New York: Wiley, 1978), p. 16. Reprinted with permission of John Wiley, Inc.

Figure 4 • Attendance, Carding Department

reduced turnover that occurred as a result of the positive atmosphere and behavior on this shift.[7]

Summary feedback is information that people receive following the performance of a task. For example, information about the number of strikes, hits, runs, and so on is essential to the major league pitcher in determining the most effective pitching strategy to use at any given point in the game. Without such feedback information, a great deal of expertise and effort can go to waste.

The effect of feedback can serve both to direct and to motivate performance in relation to a goal. For example, people who are behind in their work, when made aware of this information, are able to increase their level of effort and work harder to meet the demands of the goal. Those individuals whose progress on a task is on target or ahead of the target have the information necessary to maintain their level of effort.

Cueing and summary feedback also provide information that can lead to strategy development or procedures for goal accomplishment if the present procedure is not effective. In sum, *feedback is necessary if goal setting is to work.*

A recent study of engineers by John Ivancevich and Tim McMahon found that performance feedback generated by the engineers themselves was usually more effective in insuring high performance than feedback provided by others.[8] In all cases supervisors assigned the goals to the engineers, but in some cases they also kept track of the engineers' progress while in other cases the engineers tracked their own progress. The better performance of the latter group may have been due to the fact that they trusted feedback they gave themselves more than that provided by others; or it may be that those who kept track of their own progress were better informed about how they were doing than those whose performance was monitored by others.

Paradoxically, new technology (e.g., computers) may offer employees the capability for monitoring their own performance more accurately and more closely—and at the same time give the organization more knowledge of how employees are performing and the capability for exerting closer control.

An article in the *Wall Street Journal* reports that Bell Industries, Shaklee Corporation, and the General Electric Company are using a computerized monitor that resembles a digital clock radio. The purpose of the monitor is to provide employees with instant readings on completed tasks and their achievement of set goals. Bell Industries finds that the units halve the usual six-month training time for lathe operators at a Sunnyvale, California, memory disc plant. Furthermore, experienced workers are now routinely exceeding production goals. The employees report self-satisfaction at being able to monitor themselves. The company anticipated but didn't get any resentment from them. But union opposition may prove to be a problem: "'Just another intrusion into workers' privacy,' an AFL-CIO man growls."[9]

Employees often do not receive feedback on their performance either during or after performance of the task. In such cases, the effectiveness of goal setting is minimal. The goal or target is practically useless if there is not enough information to keep performance on track.

The timing of feedback is important in determining its effectiveness. Learning theorists have long recognized the benefits of rapid feedback, which enables an individual to evaluate and control his or her behavior on an ongoing basis. As deviations in desired behavior occur and are identified through feedback, the source of the problem is more readily identified and corrections can be made immediately. But too long a delay in providing feedback obscures the relationships between particular behaviors and their outcomes, thus blocking the resolution of performance deficiencies.

Feedback is necessary not only at the individual or work group level but also at higher organizational levels. As noted previously with regard to action plans, the complexity of controlling and coordinating organizational activity increases as one rises in the organizational hierarchy. For this reason, formal information and control systems such as accounting, performance appraisal surveys, and efficiency ratings are needed to keep track of progress toward goals. This information can assist management in planning if the data are relevant, ongoing, and timely. If performance is unsatisfactory, management can modify its activity to correct for deficiencies or possibly modify its goals if information reveals that the present course of action is not successful.

Feedback systems are most effective when the information they provide is communicated both upward and downward in the organization. For example, a formal performance appraisal system can both show management whether employees are meeting performance objectives and also identify areas where improvements are needed. However, if this appraisal is not communicated to the people actually engaged in the activity being evaluated, little improvement can be expected (see Chapter 7).

Performance feedback enables the individual to experience satisfaction with goal attainment, thus motivating him or her by indicating that continued performance will lead to further satisfaction.[10]

Another positive effect of feedback systems is that they show employees that upper management cares about them. Surveys of employee attitudes often reveal that the simple fact that a survey was conducted and that results were fed back reinforces the employees' belief that management is concerned about them.

Formal information and control systems enable management to keep track of a great deal of complex activity. However, such feedback systems, if poorly developed and implemented, can have very bad results. Often, in order to condense the amount of information flowing to management, a single criterion is selected as an indicator of performance toward an objective. The hazard of such an approach is that it may be simplistic, not allowing for a comprehensive analysis of the causes of poor performance. Further, such an approach often ignores the importance of subsidiary goals and throws the system out of balance. An example of the dysfunctional effects of a formal management feedback system is provided by Jasinsky in his classic article on the use and misuse of efficiency controls.

> Because management in this company paid so much attention to the end-of-month efficiency ratings, department supervisors left no stone unturned to get as many units into finished stores as possible. They even resorted to such expensive and disruptive processes as "bleeding the line"—that is, stopping operations near the start of the cycle and shifting labor to final operations in order to complete more units by the deadline. This process is summarized by what another foreman said:
>
> "For the last two weeks of the month we're driving hell out of the men. We have to get pieces out, and we're always jammed up at the end of the month. . . . What actually happens is that in the beginning of the month I have to put all of my men at the beginning of the line to get pieces going for the month's production. This is because

we cleaned out the department in the previous month. Then, during the last two weeks I have to put all of the men at the end of the line to finish up the pieces.

"What we should be doing is to have each man work on his machine. At the end of the month we should have a piece in each machine—not cleaned out the way we are. That way we could keep a steady flow all month and not have the rush at the end of the month."[11]

The irregular flow resulting from this process of bleeding the line in one department generated still more scheduling jams in departments to which the work pieces went later. Jasinsky describes numerous other cases where the overreliance on one measure of performance (efficiency ratings) led to such problems as increased production and maintenance costs, low morale, lowered quality and irregular or inadequate output, cynicism or dishonesty on the part of employees and supervisory personnel, and interdepartmental friction. As can be seen from the above example, the selection of performance criteria is critical. If one criterion is too simplistic, it can result in the subversion of real effectiveness, and goal attainment can be translated into simply "looking good."

Not only are management feedback systems often simplistic, but the procedure frequently becomes mechanized, rigid, and bureaucratic as important supplementary sources of information are ignored. The most vital resources of any organization are its human resources. In addition to supplying the labor that makes the organization run, employees are a valuable source of information, experience, and advice. Employees are intimately aware of the "nuts and bolts" operation of their particular jobs. They know the problems of obstacles to goal attainment in day-to-day, week-to-week, and month-to-month operations. Two-way communication forums such as teambuilding and quality circles can clarify where improvements are needed and why. Regular feedback meetings at and between all levels of the organization can describe progress toward goals, uncover problems, suggest solutions, and provide a greater awareness of the linkages among organization members and their functions.

TRAINING

As noted in the previous chapter, for goal setting to be effective the employee must have the requisite knowledge and skill. Motivation of the highest degree is of little use if employees are not technically capable of fulfilling job requirements, and it may even be detrimental if people are expending a high degree of energy doing things incorrectly.

Typically, training experts advocate an ongoing three-level process for identifying training needs in complex organizations. The first stage consists of an organization analysis, examining the organization's short- and long-term objectives, its resources, the allocation of its resources toward the accomplishment of objectives, and the broad socio-economic-technological environment within which the organization operates. The organizational analysis helps to shape the basic training philosophy for the entire organization and determines where in the organization training activities are needed, and if such activities are likely to be effective.

In the second stage of identifying training needs, a task or job analysis is conducted to identify and study specific jobs within the organization and further define the specific content of training needed. The task analysis requires a detailed and systematic collection of information about the job in order to specify what tasks make up the job, how they are performed, and what level of knowledge and skills the employee must have to perform them.

The final stage consists of a manpower analysis, which is concerned with the individual employee in a particular job, as opposed to the job itself. Both Bass and Vaughn, and Wexley and Latham discuss three basic issues that are involved in a manpower analysis for training purposes.

> First, through appropriate observation, supervisory evaluation, and diagnostic testing, we need to determine

whether performance is substandard and training is needed. Second, we need to know whether current employees are capable of training, and we need to know the specific areas in which they may require training, in order to minimize training time. Finally, we need to ask whether current employees with substandard performance can improve their work through appropriate training or should be transferred to make room for those who can already do the job. At the same time, we must consider whether engineering modifications in the job may bring employee performance up to standard, whether, instead, new equipment or processes may be the solution, or whether training seems the wisest course.[12]

Systematically following these three steps in identifying training needs is a rather expensive and rigorous enterprise. To be fully effective, the process should be performed continuously so as to be flexible enough to meet the needs of changing organizational and environmental circumstances. The process, however, need not (indeed, should not) be relegated to the personnel department alone. The basic mechanisms for identifying training needs and implementing appropriate training have already been described in this chapter. Specifically, the careful specification of goals and the action plans needed to attain them can identify relevant knowledge or skill deficiencies that may obstruct goal attainment. Furthermore, the use of comprehensive, accurate feedback systems can show management precisely where problem areas are. In addition, detailed feedback in and of itself is a critical necessity if learning is to occur and if the training process is to be effective.

Of critical importance to management, bearing directly on organizational effectiveness, is the skill of problem analysis and decision-making. Skill in these areas is essential to developing viable, specific goals and outlining the means to attain them. Although specialized technical knowledge is desirable, it is not the only key to success in these areas. Systematic problem analysis and rational, effective decision-making are also needed. These skills *can* be taught. For example, Kepner and Tregoe[13] have had wide success in training managers in these skills in numerous large corporations, such as General Motors, Ford, Du Pont, General Electric, IBM, and Honeywell.

Kepner and Tregoe maintain that training in the utilization of information is most important for improving problem-solving and decision-making performance. They employ a three-part training method which utilizes three basic principles of learning, namely, active participation, practice, and feedback of results, to maximize the understanding, retention, and transfer of the learned skills back on the job. Briefly, the first part of their training program involves the study of concepts that apply to all problem-solving and decision-making situations. The second part involves intensive practice of the concepts and procedures in a simulated business situation. The third part involves detailed and specific feedback sessions on actual performance to suggest means of improvement where necessary.

Another very powerful, but frequently overlooked, method for training and development is behavioral modeling. This technique recognizes the influence that the behavior of models (e.g., supervisors, peers) can have on the behaviors and attitudes of others.[14] One great practical benefit in recognizing modeling effects is that training and development occur day in and day out on the job to the extent that supervisors engage in appropriate goal-related behaviors and reward their subordinates for imitating such behaviors.

A study by Rakestraw and Weiss showed the utility of behavioral modeling in influencing individuals' task goals and performance.[15] They found that observation of a model's achievements had a significant effect on the goals and performance of people without prior task experience, but had less influence on the goals and performance of people who were familiar with the task before being exposed to the model. However, regardless of task familiarity, all the people used the model as a standard for evaluating their own performance. Thus careful attention to engaging in and rewarding appropriate behaviors can have a significant effect on the aspirations of individuals and the groups in which they work.

While training can help to set and achieve goals, goals at

the same time can be used to facilitate the effectiveness of training. Field experiments have investigated the usefulness of goal setting to help achieve the objectives of several management training programs. For example, Wexley and Nemeroff compared a managerial training program to a control group that received no training.[16] The program involved role playing together with follow-up appraisal sessions and assigned goals. The results showed that the program was effective in improving managerial behaviors and reducing the absenteeism of subordinates. There was no change in the control group on these variables.

In addition, Nemeroff and Cosentino conducted an experiment to improve the way managers handle performance appraisal interviews with their subordinates.[17] The training approach involved feedback plus goal setting for specific desired behaviors; another group received no training and served as a control group. The results showed that the feedback plus goal setting conditions was successful in training managers in interviewing skills.

COMPANY POLICIES

Company polices also have a tremendous influence on the effectiveness of goal setting. Policies are guidelines to action that have been established to speed up decision-making and facilitate the attainment of organization objectives. There are some similarities in the characteristics of policies and the characteristics of action plans discussed previously. Like action plans, policies vary in their breadth and scope throughout the organizational hierarchy: the further down an organization pyramid the policy occurs, the more narrow and specific it becomes. At the lowest organizational levels, policies can be viewed as simple rules to be followed. Policies also serve an important controlling function within the organization, restricting deviations from established procedures. In addition, policies establish an organizational climate because they represent the thinking of the individuals who originated them and are frequently difficult to change. Policies that are not regularly reviewed and modified to fit changing organizational requirements can actually impair an organization's ability to attain goals.

Recall the study cited in Chapter 1 that found that goal setting was the single most frequently mentioned factor leading to higher productivity for three groups of employees in one plant of a multinational firm. Of relevance here is the fact that this study also found that goal blockage was the single most frequently mentioned factor leading to low productivity.[18]

Unlike action plans, policies are fixed guides to action, inherently insensitive and unresponsive to variations in the situations they were developed to handle. An accumulation of outmoded policies is a symptom of an authoritarian, uncaring, and inflexible style of management that can harm employee morale and creativity. In addition, two-way communication between employees and management can become severely restricted, and numerous blocks to goal attainment may remain unidentified and unremedied.

The foregoing paragraph may be a "worst case" scenario. Nevertheless, it happens fairly often in many organizations in varying degrees. Herein lies the power of developing action plans and periodic performance evaluations. A general policy that builds in flexibility in organizational functioning through action plans can keep other policies under continual review.

RESOURCES

The availability and allocation of organizational resources is a fifth condition that can affect the success of a goal setting program. Without adequate money, equipment, time, or help, the attempt to achieve objectives can easily become an exercise in futility. This leads us to Chapter 7, where we discuss the importance of performance appraisals regarding such issues as the difficulty of the goal, the path or paths to be taken to attain those goals, and the obstacles that need to be removed in following a given path or set of paths to the goal.

SUMMARY

For goal setting to be effective, action plans, feedback, training, facilitative company policies, and the resources of time, money, and assistance are all necessary. Action plans are needed to guide both short- and long-term efforts in reaching the goal; emphasis here is placed on the "how" of goal attainment. Feedback is necessary to track progress toward the goal, so the person knows whether to adjust effort or strategy. Training is crucial to goal attainment—if the employee lacks skill in the areas for which the goals are set, action plans will be meaningless. Feedback will be of value here to the extent that it reveals the need for training. To get proper training, to set proper goals, and to engage in efficient action to attain those goals requires time, money, and help. Organizational policies must encourage two-way communication and the elimination of blocks to goal accomplishment.

7 • Goal setting and performance appraisal

Performance appraisals serve as a basis for decisions regarding promotion, demotion, transfer, or layoff. Frequently they are used to determine what, if any, salary increase or bonus an individual will receive. The appraisal interview is designed, in theory, to motivate and stimulate the development of the individual's strengths and correct any weaknesses, so that the person is of maximum value to the organization. In practice, however, performance appraisals sometimes reduce performance to a level lower than where it was prior to the appraisal. Furthermore, these declines in performance can last several months or longer. This was the conclusion of a now classic study conducted at the General Electric Company.[1]

The cause of these performance declines was found to be the one element that all the appraisals had in common, namely, *criticism*. And the evidence indicates that it does not matter whether the criticism comes first or last or is sandwiched in between praise.[2] Criticism typically threatens the self-esteem of subordinates. This is especially true for those who have less than average self-esteem to start with. To protect what self-esteem they have, people will frequently attack the appraiser (e.g., "If you'd get out of your office more often you'd see what I'm doing"; or "You can't perform your own job, so how can you be qualified to assess me?").[3] As a result, the subordinate pays little attention to the performance problems that do exist.

One way to escape this problem is to ignore all negative

aspects of the employee's performance, but this would simply ensure that poor performance would not be improved. A more drastic solution is to take note of deficiencies but not have any formal appraisals done at all—a practice followed by a surprisingly large number of managers. However, not giving employees feedback through an appraisal can prove costly. Feedback is necessary for improving performance. In fact, evidence indicates that little learning occurs without feedback or knowledge of results.[4] Furthermore, as noted previously, feedback is a necessary condition for the setting of goals and the monitoring of progress toward their attainment.

The failure to communicate an appraisal to a subordinate can also prove costly from a legal standpoint. A performance appraisal, regardless of whether it is communicated to the employee, is a "test" in the eyes of the law.[5] Governmental agencies such as the Equal Employment Opportunity Commission (EEOC) and the Office of Federal Contract Compliance Programs (OFCCP), as well as the Supreme Court, define a "test" as *any* decision, formal or informal, that affects an individual's status in the organization regarding selection, promotion, demotion, transfer, pay, or admission into a training program that would affect any of the foregoing. Further, this broad definition of the word "test" includes any decision-making device (e.g., a conversation at lunch) for terminating an employee.

If an employee alleges that a decision that affects him or her adversely was made on the basis of age, race, sex, religion, or national origin (age, race, and sex today are especially scrutinized by the government), the organization must be able to document the accuracy of the decision. The following incident demonstrates the necessity for such documentation.

The case involved a 56-year-old laboratory technician in a midwestern manufacturing company. The person charged that he was terminated because of his age. His employer stated that even though the man had been employed for a long time, the quality of his work was consistently poor and his attitude and rate of attendance had been unsatisfactory. The company further claimed that the man had been advised repeatedly of the company's dissatisfaction with his work before he had been fired.

In court, the employee responded that his work, in fact, had always been acceptable, that his attitude had always been good, and that he had never been advised that the company was not pleased with his work. He further stated that *he had received regular pay increases.*

The court ruled in favor of the employee. The company was ordered to give the man back his job and to pay him back wages and legal costs because the company could not offer sufficient written documentation that the employee's work performance had been bad enough to warrant discharge. The attendance records could not prove that his attendance was poor. The employee's personnel file contained no evidence that he had ever been considered to be a poor worker, or that he had been spoken to by his supervisor about unacceptable work. The only thing the file indicated was that this person had received regular pay increases.[6]

Thus inadequate performance appraisals not only can impede learning, they can also lead to costly litigation battles. In this chapter we explain how performance appraisal with an emphasis on goal setting can increase productivity and simultaneously reduce the probability of a court case being decided in favor of the plaintiff. The emphasis on goal setting is based on findings from the same General Electric study discussed earlier as well as on our own research. Taken together, this evidence shows that the most effective remedy for poor performance is to focus on the future rather than on the past. Focusing on the past is generally unproductive for two reasons: first, there is no way that the past can be undone; second, it is likely to lead to arguments due to different perceptions of past events by the supervisor and the subordinate. It is true that valuable lessons can be learned from past mistakes, but the lessons are likely to be more palatable to the learner if the emphasis is on what he or she will do differently starting tomorrow than if the emphasis is solely on the employee's past errors, omissions, and foul-ups.

MEASURING PERFORMANCE

Before one can set goals for future performance, agreement must be reached on how the employee's performance is to be assessed. An individual employee's performance can be measured in at least three ways: (1) on the basis of general traits or stable personality predispositions; (2) by outcomes or results achieved; and/or (3) on the basis of observed behavior.

Most organizations assess people on the basis of traits, examples of which include initiative, cooperation, loyalty, and attitude. The advantage of this approach may explain its popularity. One appraisal form can generally be developed for all employees in all settings. Every president wants a clerk as well as a vice president to show initiative, to cooperate with others, to be loyal to the company, and to display a good attitude.

The disadvantages of this approach are primarily twofold. First, the words are vague and ambiguous because they are seldom if ever defined in terms of the explicit behaviors that must be demonstrated to get a favorable appraisal. Goal setting is difficult when traits are involved, because the employee may set goals that contradict the manager's definition of the traits in question.

For example, a supervisor in one organization was told to be a "better listener." So he set a goal for remaining silent at staff meetings on the premise that the boss wanted less discussion. In fact, staff meetings had no relation to the comment on listening. The comment actually referred to better understanding the needs of clients. In a subsequent appraisal, the same employee received low ratings because of "poor listening skills" and "lack of initiative in self-development."

Why should such an absurd incident occur? Because "listening better to clients" was never clearly defined by the supervisor, so the subordinate made his own interpretation, which happened to conflict with that of his boss!

A second problem with traits is that their vagueness and ambiguity may cause the organization to lose a court case if an employment decision is challenged by the employee.[7] The courts have ruled repeatedly that trait scales are susceptible to the personal taste, whim, or fancy of the evaluator.

Due to the weaknesses of trait scales, many managers prefer to use measured work results or work outcomes to appraise employees. As noted in Chapter 4, outcome measures are of three basic types: physical units (e.g., amount produced, number sold); time-related measures (meeting deadlines); and outcomes measured in monetary terms (sales, costs, profits, and so on). Such measures make quite explicit what it is the employee is to accomplish. They are objective, and they focus on one employee's impact. They also lend themselves to the setting of specific difficult goals, which in turn can lead to large increases in performance. However, certain cautions must be observed when using outcome measures.

First, these outcomes must be under the control of the employee, regardless of whether the employee is the company president or a filing clerk. If factors beyond the control of the individual affect the outcome adversely, appraisals made on that basis will at best demotivate the employee and at worst could be challenged successfully in court. On the other hand, if factors beyond the control of the employee affect the outcome positively (e.g., high sales in a booming economy), the organization must be certain not to let these outcomes unduly influence the appraisal (sales *might* have increased regardless of, or even in spite of, the sales manager).

For example, at the huge LTV Corporation headquarters in Dallas, Texas, much of their effort at year-end is spent dealing with:

> . . . an assessment of the environment in which the results were achieved—problem by problem—company by company—individual by individual. To illustrate, one of our companies exceeded their profit objectives, which was judged to be an easy task in light of the environment. Although falling short of profitability goals, another company was judged to have performed very well under the circumstances. The quality of the results, therefore, is

largely a function of the environment which existed during the period. To some extent the environment can, and should, be predictable. But unexpected problems and opportunities to overcome or seize, as the case may be, will arise and impact results. One outcome of this evaluation process is a compensation reward which is performance related, and not just results related. We have found that our executives endorse this concept as being a better reflection of their efforts than our previous formula-driven reward practices based solely on outcomes.[8]

A second caution in using outcome measures is that the outcomes on different jobs or units must not be in conflict. For example, the raw materials department of a wood products company may send expensive chips from a valued supplier to the pulpmill in order to make sure that its monthly income statements look good and because this will ensure good service in the future from this supplier. The immediate result, however, may be that the statements of the pulpmill would look bad because of the high cost charged to them for the chips they processed. Consequently, the pulpmill's quality-control people may find ingenious ways of rejecting the chips. This is especially likely to happen if the pulpmill has been told to "reduce costs this quarter." Clearly there is a need to integrate the various goals here in a way that benefits the company as a whole.

Third, it should be noted that it is not always feasible or cost-effective to obtain outcome measures for all employees. Even if such measures could be obtained, it may not be worth the time and trouble to do so.

Fourth, one must be careful that outcome measures do not encourage a "results-at-all-costs" mentality where the end is everything and the means are overlooked. This type of thinking can lead to undesirable short cuts and unethical practices. The organization, in addition to undermining employee morale, may even end up in court as a result of the latter.

Finally, cost-related variables such as "units produced/employee hours worked" tell the employee whether the "game is being won or lost," but they give little or no information on how to start or how to continue winning. Thus, they are of little or no value as a basis for coaching and developing an employee. Consequently, industrial psychologists as well as the courts emphasize the need to identify the key or critical behaviors an individual in a given position (e.g., secretary) or family of positions (e.g., all clerical jobs) needs to demonstrate on the job in order to affect outcome measures.

When outcome measures are not readily available, or when developing them is not cost effective, the organization may instead use behavioral measures. As noted in Chapter 4, these are chosen on the premise that certain types of actions will ultimately lead to desirable outcomes. One type of behavioral measure, the Behavioral Observation Scale (BOS), was described in Chapter 4. As shown in Figure 3 on p. 29, scores on individual items of BOS scales can be summed to form total scores, and these total scores can be used as a basis for setting goals. For example, an employee could be told that a minimally acceptable score was 160 out of a possible 200 (after summing the scores on all scales).

A primary disadvantage of using behavioral measures is that it is unlikely in all but the smallest organizations that one appraisal instrument will be sufficient for all employees regardless of their job position. Thus it may be necessary to spend a substantial amount of time on developing multiple forms—one for each job category or family (e.g., managers, professionals, technicians, sales workers, clerical workers, and skilled craftspeople). This disadvantage may be more than offset, however, by the counseling value of an instrument that is tailor-made for the job or job family in question. Further, it minimizes the possibility that a job incumbent will reject the appraisal because the instrument omits important areas for which he or she is accountable.

Another disadvantage of BOS is the very fact that they are based on the observations of one or more observers rather than on direct measurements. Thus, they are subject to potential biases and inaccuracies. While the BOS format is a substantial improvement over trait scales, it is important that observers receive training in ways to improve their objectivity and accuracy in recording what they see.

It should be noted that one does not necessarily have to choose between outcome measures and behavioral measures, since it is often possible to use both for a given job. Those aspects of performance for which reasonable outcome measures exist should be used along with behavioral measures. In this way the ends as well as the means by which the ends were achieved, are evaluated.

To decide what aspects of the job are crucial enough to warrant evaluation or appraisal of performance, a job analysis should be conducted to identify what is truly critical to the success of the organization, department, and/or individual. This is typically done through a consensus involving employees and their superiors, and in some instances subordinates and clients. The analysis typically focuses on leverage points critical to the success of the department or organization as a whole.

It should also be stressed that while outcome measures typically come from one source (e.g., organizational records), behavioral measures should be obtained from multiple sources. Traditionally, employee evaluations have been based solely on the observations of the employee's immediate boss. While this is an invaluable source of information, the boss may not always have the full picture. He or she is often busy with work that does not involve direct observation of a given subordinate, and there may be many different subordinates to keep track of. To supplement the immediate supervisor's information, observations can also be obtained from the employee's peers, from other supervisors or managers who deal with the employee, and from the employee's subordinates (if there are any). Of course, biases can occur in each case: co-workers may want to make themselves look good at their colleague's expense; a subordinate may hold a grudge for failing to get an undeserved pay raise; or other managers may not like this employee's manager. However, the immediate supervisor may also be biased. The advantages of using multiple raters are that: (1) there is more information than in the case with a single observer; and

(2) blatant biases and differences of interpretation can be uncovered by examining contradictions among the evaluations from different sources. For this purpose it is also useful to have more than one person integrating all the information in order to make the final overall appraisal.

CONDUCTING APPRAISAL INTERVIEWS

Before conducting an appraisal interview, the manager should have available the overall appraisal and the facts to back it up. The manager may also want to have the employee perform a self-appraisal on the BOS before the meeting. If there is agreement between the two, this saves a lot of time and permits the interview to proceed toward setting specific goals for the future. On the other hand, if there are substantial disagreements, the supervisor and the subordinate can spend time discussing possible reasons for the disagreements (which may involve selective memory, differing interpretations of the same events, differing opinions about what goals were to be achieved) and agree on ways of resolving them.

Certain guidelines should be followed in conducting the appraisal interview [9]:

1. Explain that the purpose of the meeting is to provide recognition for areas in which the employee is doing well and to discuss any problems that the employee may be experiencing on the job. The employee should be given sufficient notice of the meeting and the questions that the supervisor will ask so that the discussion is not one-sided.

2. At the beginning of the meeting, ask the employee to describe to you what he or she has done that deserves recognition, and how it was done. Take notes. Do not comment if you disagree with what is being said. Disagreement at this stage may inhibit further employee discussion. You should simply listen.

3. Ask the employee if there are areas on the job where you can provide assistance. In this way you are showing that you truly want to help.

4. Clearly describe to the employee what he or she has done that you believe deserves recognition. Be specific so the employee knows exactly what needs to be done to maintain this appreciation. The advantages of specificity are that it is meaningful to an employee and it increases the probability that the desired behavior will be repeated. It minimizes feelings of favoritism if other employees hear specifically why one individual was praised and if they too are praised for engaging in the same behavior. It increases the probability that the listener will understand that the praise is sincere because the listener knows that he or she did in fact do "such and such." If there is a surprise on the part of the listener, it is the fact that the supervisor noticed the behavior and took the time to comment upon it. The disadvantages of giving praise in terms of generalities (e.g., "You are doing a super job.") are the opposite of the preceding. The praise becomes meaningless and may be seen as insincere. In addition, the praise may inadvertently encourage some of the very behaviors that you, the supervisor, wishes the employee would stop doing. The supervisor needs to say, "You are doing a super job because. . . ."

5. If the employee fails to mention areas that you feel are important, discuss no more than two broad aspects of performance where you feel improvement is needed. Research has shown that focusing on more than two aspects can overwhelm an employee and increase defensiveness. Focus strictly on the problems and not on personalities. Simply explain what you have seen and why it concerns you. There is no question that any evaluative process can be threatening to some employees. However, when the appropriate behaviors are well-known to both the employee and the supervisor, and when the measurement of these behaviors is discussed openly, anxiety is reduced and the relationship between the employee and the supervisor can become frank and comfortable. This is another reason why objective performance measures are so important as appraisal instruments. They make it clear to all parties what is required of an employee.

6. Ask for and listen openly to the employee's concerns. These may require your attention.

7. Come to agreement on the specific steps to be taken by both of you, especially in regard to future behaviors that are to be demonstrated and objectives that are to be obtained. Specify these steps in the form of specific, challenging goals. If outcome

measures are used, agree on a specific score that the employee will strive to attain on the next appraisal. If behavioral measures are used, agree on the frequency with which the employee will demonstrate the behavior(s) in terms of the score on a specific scale.

8. Finally, agree on a follow-up date to determine the extent to which the employee's and your concerns have been eliminated and to see if progress has been made on the goals that have been set.

Periodic follow-up meetings should occur within appraisal periods to review the relevance of the agreed-on goals; to discuss obstacles, if any, preventing goal attainment if the goal or goals are still relevant; and to provide praise for behaviors demonstrated and/or results accomplished. Conducting an appraisal only once a year is about as effective as taking only one tennis or golf lesson in a year. It may make the person aware of poor habits, but it is unlikely to bring about and sustain effective behavior. Similarly, setting only long-range goals is not as effective as setting subgoals that are to be attained in order to reach the long-range goals. Periodic feedback is needed to reinforce the employee's efforts if goals are being attained, or to provide an opportunity for problem-solving if goals are being missed.

In summary, goal setting, with its emphasis on the future, can be an extremely effective and cost-efficient way to improve employee performance. The study done at General Electric found that goal setting during performance appraisal was a key factor in changing future performance.[10] For example, they discovered that of the aspects of performance that were translated into specific goals, 65 percent showed subsequent improvement; in contrast, among aspects for which no goals were set, only 27 percent showed later improvement. Two studies described below further verify these findings.

Motivating R & D professionals to improve their performance [11]. Because of the severity of the economic recession, the president of a large international company formed a task force consisting of line vice presidents and managers to identify ways of reducing costs. The task force concluded that significant savings could be obtained by reducing, if not eliminating, the company's research and development (R & D) staff.

The senior vice president of R & D countered this proposal with a challenge: if he were allowed to keep the R & D group intact for one year, he would assure the company that R & D would become invaluable to line management. This counterproposal was accepted by the president. A second task force was formed to examine ways of increasing the value of R & D people to the company.

Within weeks, the second task force was bogged down. No progress was being made. The members argued whether motivation was or was not a problem among the department's highly paid, highly educated scientists and engineers. They also worried about whether the problem was simply one of communication between line and R & D management. Others argued that the problem was insurmountable because it was imbedded in larger issues, including the role, if any, of R & D in the private sector, the deep-seated prejudices of line people who want R & D to initiate only those projects that would affect profits immediately, and so on.

The problems facing this task force appeared to be growing daily, until someone asked two simple questions. What is it we want R & D people to do? How can we motivate them to do anything differently until we answer that question?

To answer the first question a job analysis was conducted. People who were aware of the aims and objectives of R & D, who frequently observed R & D people on the job, and who could discern competent from incompetent performance were asked to do the following: "Think back over the past six to twelve months of an incident where you yourself observed an engineer/scientist who did something effective or ineffective. The person's name should not be identified. Simply report (a) what the circumstances were that surrounded the incident that you observed; (b) the exact behavior that you observed on the part of the engineer or scientist; and (c) how or why this incident is an example of effective/ineffective behavior." The result of this job analysis was an exhaustive list of dos and don'ts for R & D people, and the task force was now ready to tackle the question of how to get R & D people to exhibit these behaviors.

It was recommended that the behavioral checklist be turned into Behavioral Observation Scales. That is, supervisors were to observe the extent to which each subordinate demonstrated the behavior on the checklist and then record the frequency of the occurrence. The observations were to be reported to the subordinate (feedback), and a specific goal was then to be assigned to the employee with regard to an overall score to obtain on the next appraisal.

BOS were duly developed, they were discussed with the scientists during an appraisal interview, and goals were set for future performance in the form of scores to be obtained on the scale. In some cases the goals were assigned and in other cases they were set jointly (i.e., participatively) by a superior and a subordinate. A control group was not given either the BOS or the goals.

The results showed a significant improvement in performance as a result of goal setting. In this study, those who set goals participatively did slightly better than those who were assigned goals because the goals set participatively were higher than those set unilaterally by the supervisor.

The final outcome was that the R & D division was kept intact. The job analysis identified the behaviors critical for functioning effectively in the organization. Goal setting and feedback helped the engineers and scientists to demonstrate those behaviors.

Improving the performance of word processing operators [12]. The word processing operators in an organization were accustomed to being appraised solely on the number of error-free words typed per minute. This resulted in the selection and retention of highly skilled individuals. Within three years, however, there was a growing dissatisfaction within management with the performance of these skilled operators. Some operators were spending an inordinate amount of time on one job, and others used the company telephone excessively for personal calls. Still other operators refused to accept client instructions or else repeatedly went back to their customer for clarification. The use of these two outcome variables (typing speed and accuracy) for appraisal purposes had not provided a comprehensive measure of operator job effectiveness as far as management was concerned.

A job analysis was conducted with the word processing operators and their supervisors to identify those behaviors that "when you saw it occur made you wish every operator would do the same thing under the same circumstances." Included among the behaviors identified as critical to an operator's effectiveness were both typing speed and accuracy. The differences here were that typing speed and accuracy were defined in terms of the behaviors that consistently led to these two outcomes (e.g., checking work for accuracy), and the list included other key factors that were also identified and defined behaviorally (e.g., cooperation with other operators, planning, commitment to job).

Once these behaviors were identified and defined, each supervisor appraised each employee on the resulting BOS. Specific performance goals were either assigned to or set participatively with each employee.

The results showed that appraisal through goal setting increased performance dramatically within four months. Participation in goal setting, however, had no greater effect on performance, goal attainment, or goal acceptance than assigning goals.

So where do these two studies leave us? Regardless of whether the goal is assigned by a supervisor or involves employee participation in the process, goal setting is an approach to performance appraisal that works.

SUMMARY

Performance appraisal serves many vital functions for an organization. However, such appraisals often lead to performance declines rather than improvements when employees are criticized and respond defensively. Avoiding this problem by abandoning performance appraisal or appraisal interviews not only ensures that performance problems will recur but may place the organization in legal jeopardy.

Performance is typically appraised in one of three ways: by the use of trait scales, by objective outcome measures, or by Behavioral Observation Scales. Trait scales are inherently ambiguous and are not recommended. Outcome measures can be extremely useful when they are available and relevant to the job. Behavioral Observation Scales are always recommended, so that the means as well as the ends receive proper attention.

To be effective an appraisal interviewer should (1) explain the purpose of the meeting; (2) ask the employee what has been done that deserves recognition; (3) ask where the employee needs assistance; (4) describe specifically what the interviewer thinks deserves recognition; (5) identify problem areas where improvement is needed; (6) ask about the employee's concerns; (7) come to agreement on the steps to be taken by each of them phrased in the form of specific goals; and (8) plan a follow-up meeting.

8 • *Goal setting and stress**

Stress is becoming the catchword of our age. Scores of books and hundreds of articles have been written about it. It is discussed on countless talk shows and at conventions. Dozens of possible cures are offered for it. Unfortunately, however, almost nobody identifies what stress is. Thus we will begin this chapter by defining this popular term.

There are four elements that define a situation as involving stress:

1. An important goal or value is blocked or threatened. To be under stress, something important to the individual must be at stake. It may be the individual's life, as in the case of a battle or a dangerous adventure, or it may be something the individual wants very much, such as a new business or success on a particular project. The value also may involve the person's self-concept or self-esteem. If there is nothing important that can be lost, then there is no stress.

Threats to goals and values can come in many forms in organizational settings. For example, a manager may not be able to reach a goal because of company policies that block goal attainment. Government regulations may prevent implementing a plan of action. The actions of competitors may make it difficult to sell a sufficient quantity of a product. A vice presi-

---

*The authors are indebted to Mr. James Carr for part of the conceptual framework on which this chapter is based.

dent may make impossible demands and threaten punishment if these demands are not satisfied.

Observe that if one is totally secure regarding the achievement or retention of one's goals or values, then there is no stress. For example, a wealthy individual with modest spending habits would feel little or no economic stress during a recession.

2. Action is required to deal with the threat. Action always implies (a) knowledge, (b) an appraisal or evaluation of that knowledge, (c) decision-making, which involves the integration of knowledge and evaluation, and (d) the consequences of the decision. All of these can entail stress because they involve commitment and the possibility of being wrong. Action implies responsibility; being wrong may lead not only to the loss of the goal or value sought, but to feelings of guilt, self-doubt, and/or self-condemnation over the outcome.

One has the choice, of course, of foregoing action and eliminating all stress, but then the goal or value is lost altogether. For example, if one were offered a challenging, difficult job, one could refuse it and stay on the old job. This would prevent further stress, but the opportunity to further develop one's skills (in that context) would be gone.

Stress is greater if the individual, based on past habits, does not trust himself to take the appropriate actions to achieve the goal when a threat occurs. If a person believes, "I will probably go to pieces when the going gets rough," this individual will feel fundamentally out of control. He experiences an increased feeling of vulnerability because he is, in fact, more vulnerable to blocks that threaten his goals and values. In contrast, a person who trusts him- or herself to carefully assess threatening situations, to develop suitable action plans, and to carry them out will not feel as threatened because the actual threat, in relation to coping skills and habits, is less.

The fundamental cause of feeling out of control under stress is the expectation, based on past habits, that one will make decisions based on emotion rather than on rational evaluation of the facts. A middle level administrator, for example, felt frightened whenever one of her subordinates did not do the job correctly. The manager knew that she was expected to take action to resolve the problem but feared that she would go to pieces at the first sign of anger or protest on the part of a subordinate. Her habit was to give in to the fear and not really handle the problem at all. Her fear diminished only when she learned what to do and say in such situations and then put that knowledge into action. By acting against her fear successfully on a number of occasions, she gradually came to feel that she was in control.

3. There is uncertainty as to the outcome. Since people are neither omniscient nor omnipotent, they cannot always know the consequences of their actions in advance. In making choices, they must live with the knowledge that things may or may not turn out in their favor.

If there were total certainty about a given outcome, there would be no stress even if the outcome were negative. For example, if a manager knew for certain that he was going to be laid off and that nothing could be done about it, he would feel no stress with regard to the layoff (although he might with respect to the consequences of the layoff, since subsequent action would be required). Similarly, if another manager were certain (due to inside information) that a promotion was forthcoming and that nothing could change that fact, then she would feel no stress over the issue of promotion (although she might with respect to the types of problems that would be encountered in the new job).

4. Anxiety. As a result of the previous three conditions, that is, the existence of a threat to one's goals, the need for action, and the uncertainty of results, the individual will experience some degree of anxiety. *Anxiety is the form in which one experiences threats to one's goals or values.*

As noted earlier, the degree of anxiety experienced is not just a matter of the objective nature of the external threat. It is a function of the individual's appraisal of that threat. In this sense stress is a function of the individual's perception of the relationship between himself and his environment. It is governed by his appraisal of obstacles in relation to his goals and values and by his ability and willingness to cope with those obstacles. Thus a situation that might seem trivial to one person (e.g., starting a new project at work) might send another into paroxysms of fear and anxiety.

Most of us, of course, must face many stressful situations in our lifetimes, e.g., an examination in school, a new job, an important project at work, a child's illness, a shortage of money, a fire, a move to a new city, a divorce, and so on. Stress may cause one or more of a variety of symptoms, both psychological and physical. Psychologically we may feel nervous, tense, afraid, worried, and not in full control. We may doubt our sense of worth or efficacy, and as a result we may wonder if we can cope with the threats that challenge us. Physically we may experience the usual anxiety symptoms in the short run (e.g., rapid pulse and breathing, tense muscles, sweating, nausea, dizziness, headaches, etc.) as well as more serious symptoms in the long run, if stress is prolonged (e.g., heart disease, cancer, ulcers, etc.). The particular physical symptoms and diseases that result will depend not only on the degree and type of stress experienced, but also on our own bodily susceptibilities.

Two broad and contrasting approaches can be taken in an attempt to alleviate stress. First, action can be taken to directly *relieve emotional symptoms,* such as relaxation training, physical exercise, consumption of alcohol and/or drugs, reliance on social supports, or the release of emotions such as hostility or withdrawal. Second, actions can be taken whose goal is to *remove the underlying causes* of stress, such as modifying one's values (alone or through counseling or therapy), taking action to decrease uncertainty, and, most important, taking action to overcome the obstacle(s).

In a study of small businesses devastated by a major flood, Professor Carl Anderson and his colleagues found that the owners who recovered most rapidly and fully from the flood damage (all other factors, such as economic resources, being equal) were those who used techniques of the second type to remove the causes of stress; those who focused on gaining emotional relief recovered much less rapidly.[1] A follow-up study found that those who successfully used task-centered coping mechanisms came to feel more in control of their lives, while those who coped poorly, using emotion centered mechanisms, came to feel less in control.[2]

GOAL CENTERED STRESS AND HOW TO ALLEVIATE IT

Since the potential sources of stress on a job are too numerous to catalogue, we will confine our discussion to those that are associated with goal setting, namely, goal difficulty, goal overload, goal conflict, and goal ambiguity.

Observe at the outset that if the organization considers goal setting to be important enough to encourage or require it, then in most instances employees will consider the goals important too. As we have seen, goals must be attained by action and, as with most human actions, the outcomes are uncertain.

In his landmark study of general managers (GMs), for example, John Kotter found that uncertainty was an inherent and unavoidable part of their job:

> Some of the GMs in this study were responsible for operations that spanned the entire globe. Some were responsible for the manufacturing and selling of hundreds of different kinds of products. Some were responsible for operations that employed many different technologies. In the case of a typical GM, thousands of people, most of whom were not physically located close to him, were somehow involved in his operations on a daily basis. . . . The most impressive information-systems technology available today cannot monitor all this activity quickly and accurately. Even if it could, a GM could spend twenty-four hours a day simply trying to digest that information. . . .
>
> Furthermore, the complex nature of the operational activities associated with most of these jobs can make it very difficult to know what to do when a "problem" is seen.[3]

Since goals are important, require action, and involve uncertainty, some degree of anxiety is inevitable. Now consider how particular aspects of the goal setting process can be a source of stress.

Goal difficulty exists when the goals are hard to reach. Such goals typically require more work (e.g., longer hours) and greater risk than easy or moderate goals. In addition, they usually require more complex strategies than goals that are easy to reach. If goals are hard, it is highly likely that obstacles will arise. Developing strategies to overcome the obstacles may involve extensive information search and evaluation and the making of numerous difficult decisions whose outcomes are uncertain. Under the pressure of difficult goals, individuals sometimes choose poor strategies. For example, they may blindly use methods that have worked well in the past without taking account of new factors in the situation. They may take foolish risks without fully considering the consequences. They may resort to short-term solutions that will be harmful in the long run.

Difficult goals also entail a greater risk of failure than less challenging goals. People like to feel the sense of achievement and efficacy that comes with success, so they have a certain vested interest in goals that are not too hard to reach. But, as noted earlier, goals that are *too* easy lead to low performance. Thus there is a trade-off between the higher performance engendered by more difficult goals, and the greater likelihood of success and satisfaction that accompanies easier goals.

It also helps to know that one will get credit for partial success rather than only for complete success. A supervisor can mitigate the stressful aspects of hard goals by being supportive, and especially by helping with strategy development. Also, employees need to be adequately trained and experienced in their specialties so that they feel efficacious. One organization found, for example, that unwanted turnover could be reduced by more than half simply by increasing training time from three-fourths of a day to two days for new employees who had to learn a complex task as soon as they were hired.[4]

As noted above, difficult goals are stressful, in part, because they imply the possibility of failure. For example, a key project may not be completed on time; a losing division may not be made profitable; a new product may not sell; a sales goal might not be met. Superficially, it might appear that such failures would reduce stress, since the uncertainty is gone. However, if one considers the wider context of the individual's life, it is evident that failure can be extremely stressful. First, it can raise uncertainties about whether the individual will be fired. Second, it can raise doubts about the individual's promotion potential in the company and about his or her career prospects in general. Third, it can lead the person to wonder whether colleagues, friends, and loved ones will show the same respect as before. Fourth, it can threaten the individual's self-concept, especially if she has always seen herself as the type of person who succeeds. In short, one failure today can pose the spectre of numerous future failures.

Several years ago, for example, the president of a corporation with sales in the millions of dollars was fired by his board of directors after making a series of very poor decisions based mainly on emotions. The president, who prided himself on being successful, was stunned—he had never failed at anything before in his life. Eventually he had a mental breakdown and had to be hospitalized for severe depression. It was years before he began to recover.

Most failures are not as traumatic as this one, but they are never pleasant. One of the best antidotes to failure is the anticipation of future success. This can be done by analyzing previous errors, lowering goals to more realistic levels, developing new skills, formulating better action plans, and taking to heart the encouragement and support, if any, offered by one's supervisor. Sometimes the solution is to transfer to a new job within the organization or even to change employers. Many executives and entrepreneurs who are eventually successful have failed in the past, but these failures gave them valuable experience in the "school of hard knocks."[5]

When goals are both very difficult and numerous (or even when they are moderately difficult but so numerous that attaining all of them is nearly impossible), the individual may suffer from *goal overload*. When there is simply too much to do, threats to goals cannot be eliminated, or at least not fast enough.

One manager who read an earlier draft of this chapter asserted indignantly that most people function at such a low percentage of their capacity that there could be no such thing as goal overload! It was, he declared, "a lazy man's concept." While we have some degree of sympathy for this viewpoint, there are clearly cases where goal overload is genuine—anyone can be overloaded if he is given enough work.

Since it is the equivalent of being assigned a very hard goal, goal overload will, up to a certain point, lead to greater accomplishment than high, medium, or low work loads. However, after this point, work quality and goal commitment may suffer, and so may the person. In mild cases, the individual may simply feel overworked. In more extreme cases he may feel overwhelmed, frightened, and helpless. He may experience an intense desire to escape from pressure through alcohol, sex, drugs, or illness. Extreme and prolonged overload can cause a person to quit the job or, if nothing is done to cope with it, it can lead to mental illness or suicide.

Consider the case of Roger Berman, a high-level manager in a multinational corporation, who became increasingly distressed as the pressures of his job steadily mounted. At age 50, after thirty years with the company, he asked to take early retirement, but the company urged him to stick with the job and promised a workload reduction. It never came. Worse yet, Roger found that he would not be eligible for early retirement for another five years. He sought psychiatric help and continued to complain about this work load, but to no avail. Finally, Berman committed suicide. His widow sued the company for $6 million.[6]

It should be noted that not all stress is externally imposed; some people deliberately seek goal overload or structure their jobs so that overload is built into it. This is especially true of what is called the *Type A* personality. The Type *A* personality syndrome is characterized by a sense of extreme time urgency, a habit of doing things (talking, eating, working) rapidly, extreme competitiveness, chronic impatience, and compulsive goal achievement, typically against quantitative standards. In a work environment that encourages such patterns, Type As may experience a high degree of stress. Research indicates that Type As are more likely to develop coronary heart disease than those who do not show this pattern.[7]

In some cases the real cause of goal overload is not having too many goals, but not utilizing one's time properly. For example, a person may lack a hierarchy of importance to direct time allocation; inadequate planning may lead to a scattergun approach to work, or to "spinning one's wheels." He or she may take up too much time with trivia while major issues remain unaddressed. Such an individual may require training in time management.

Overload can also be eased by delegating more work to subordinates. Failure to delegate can result from a lack of confidence in the ability of subordinates to perform certain tasks, but in other cases it is just a matter of insecurity. Often this is mislabeled an ego problem, when actually it is a *lack of* ego problem: the individual is too insecure to admit that he or she cannot do everything without help. A manager may have a perfectionist streak that will not allow delegation of anything that will not be done perfectly (perfection often being defined as "the way I would do it"). Highly competent managers seldom remember the fact that *they* could do almost anything that many subordinates do, and better or faster to boot, is precisely why they *are* the bosses and their subordinates are subordinates! Nevertheless, it is simply more efficient for a manager to delegate everything that a subordinate can do reasonably well in order to free up the manager's time for more important tasks.

When the problem is not one of time management or inadequate delegation of work, another possible solution is that the time frame may need to be extended. Stretch out the deadlines for tasks or goals that can be postponed, even if it means that some tasks will be temporarily ignored so that full attention can be devoted to the more urgent problems.

Barring any of the above solutions, the individual will require more support, especially in the way of resources, including other people. However, goal overload can often simply be tolerated if the individual has a high capacity for dealing with overload, or if the situation will not be permanent. People can put up with a lot of stress if they know that there is a definite time when it will end or at least be reduced.

Another source of stress in goal setting is *goal conflict*, which may create incompatible action tendencies and make a threat seem uncontrollable. Goal conflicts may involve clashes between the individual's personal values and goals and the demands or assigned goals of the job (e.g., an advertising agent with antinuclear bias being asked to do an ad campaign for a utility that uses nuclear reactors). More often, however, goal conflicts occur when one is assigned clashing or incompatible goals, either by the same person or by different people. For instance, there may be intense pressure to attain an unusually high level of productivity and at the same time maintain perfect quality; or the individual's immediate boss may demand that top priority be given to goal X while the boss's boss wants goal Y attained before all else. This is clearly a no-win situation. If goal X is put first, one person will be happy and the other will be angry. If goal Y is given priority, the opposite will occur. The only feasible solution in such a case is to ask for a meeting with both bosses, indicate what the problem is, and try to come up with a solution that will satisfy everyone.

At the highest corporate level (and to a lesser degree at lower levels), a certain degree of conflict is built into the job. For example, the CEO is supposed to please the stockholders, the board of directors, government regulators, the unions, middle managers, the rank and file, and others. While the ultimate best interests of all parties may be the same, in that no one will benefit if the organization is not productive and profitable, in the short run there are bound to be some disagreements regarding both goals and strategies for reaching those goals. However, if the CEO has a clear sense of purpose and is successful in achieving it, much potential criticism will be muted.

A further potential source of stress on the job is *goal ambi-*

guity, which occurs when goals are not clear. In this situation the element of uncertainty, a key element of the stress situation, is at its maximum. For example, the individual may have no goals at all other than subtle guidelines based on frowns and smiles from the boss, or the goals may be so vague in nature (e.g., "do your best") that it is impossible to direct actions toward anything specific. The solution to this problem, as we have indicated earlier, is to set specific, preferably quantitative or verifiable, goals.

GOALS AS STRESS REDUCERS

It should not be inferred from the foregoing that goals always increase stress, for they also function as stress reducers or preventers. If a person knows clearly what is expected on the job, including the standard(s) against which he or she will be evaluated, an important potential source of uncertainty is eliminated.

Furthermore, when goals, especially difficult ones, are attained, the individual not only feels satisfaction over a job well done but pride in accomplishment. If the task requires, as most do, the productive use of the individual's mind, success heightens self-esteem. This is as true for the CEO who turns a declining company around as it is for the unskilled, unemployed worker who masters his or her first job skill. When people succeed, they feel an increased sense of efficacy—they feel, in the context of their work, that they can cope, that they can master reality. The conviction that they are competent lessens the threat posed by future assignments and makes people more willing to take on challenging tasks in the future.

For an individual to feel confident in reaching a goal, he or she must have sufficient ability and knowledge. As noted in previous chapters, knowledge is insured (given proper selection techniques) by adequate training and experience on the job. It is also important for the individual to be given the right job for his or her talents.

STAGES IN DECISION-MAKING

In the case of goals requiring the creation of appropriate task strategies or action plans, additional skills, including decision-making skills, may be needed. Daniel Wheeler and Irving Janis argue that there are five stages involved in effective decision-making.[8] We have formulated each of them as they apply specifically to the goal setting or implementation processes.

1. Effective decision-makers accept the challenge posed by a problem or a potential problem. Ineffective decision-makers procrastinate or rationalize problems away. For example, a major mini-computer manufacturer was aware for a period of five years that their competitors might be developing a new "super-mini" that could seriously cut into their business. The company did nothing. Inevitably, one day a much larger competitor announced that it had developed just such a machine. The smaller company was at first paralyzed. Only an heroic effort by a small group of brilliant young engineers, who developed a competing machine in a little over a year, saved the company from disaster. While the machine eventually became a great success, the company lost millions of dollars in potential sales during the year and a half in which the competitor had the field to itself.[9]

Effective decision-makers do not wait for external conditions to force them to set goals; instead, they anticipate problems. They rate potential problems as to their seriousness and their likelihood of occurrence and they develop appropriate objectives and plans.

2. Effective decision-makers consider a wide range of alternatives when making decisions to implement goals. Ineffective decision-makers, on the other hand, impulsively choose the first alternative that comes to mind or stop considering alternatives before their minimum criteria are met. For example, a nationwide manufacturer lost its regional sales manager, and the goal was to find a replacement in a hurry. The firm considered a dozen candidates but none met the standards. Since they did not want to wait any longer, they hired the best of the lot, but he failed and the company lost business as a result. When it went looking again, this time without insisting on a quick solution, however, the firm found the right man.

Very few decisions are really so urgent that a fast but dubious decision is better than a slow but sound one. Sometimes thinking of alternatives requires "thinking outside the square," i.e., looking for nonobvious solutions. Consider, for example, the problem of what to do with a manager who has just been promoted but is not doing the job successfully. The most obvious solution is to fire the manager—but consider other possibilities. Perhaps the manager does not really understand what is expected and only needs clearer objectives, or maybe he or she needs additional training. If the manager has a record of past success, the solution may be to match him or her to the right job through demotion or lateral transfer. The greater the number of alternatives considered (within reason), the greater the likelihood of finding a satisfactory solution.

3. Effective decision-makers evaluate alternatives according to specific, predetermined standards or criteria, both short- and long-term. Ineffective decision-makers fail to anticipate the major consequences of their decisions or fail to get adequate information regarding the probable consequences. Consider the case of the food manufacturer whose goal was to develop a new "instant" dessert. The initial market-testing looked extremely promising, but to save money it was necessary to change the recipe somewhat before the product was marketed. The company was so confident of the success of the product that it did not perform a final test marketing, the standard procedure for introducing new products. The product did not sell, and the company lost millions of dollars because of the failure to perform a complete evaluation of the new product.

When there are several alternatives that are worth considering seriously, evaluate all of them against the predetermined standards. For better results, use a *decisional balance sheet* that lists all of the outcomes and standards and assigns appropriate point values proportional to the importance of the outcome or standard. Then rate each alternative against each standard (by assigning the appropriate number of points) and total the points for each alternative.

4. Effective decision-makers develop contingency plans in case important plans do not work out. Less effective decision-makers fail to anticipate problems or setbacks. Take the case of a paper manufacturer who made heavy, high quality paper used by prestige magazines. The product sold as fast as the firm could make it, and profits soared. Despite warnings of a rise in postal rates (the postal service had considered it several times already), the potential effects of such a rise on sales were not considered. When the postal service finally did increase rates, customers immediately demanded a lighter weight paper in order to keep down their mailing costs. The company's goal was to give their customers what they wanted, but how could it? There was no lightweight paper available! As a result, the company lost 70 percent of its business within two weeks. Competing companies had developed lighter papers and were ready when the demand for them jumped.[10]

5. Effective decision-makers do not panic when obstacles arise during the implementation of a decision. They develop plans to overcome setbacks. When necessary, they go through the entire decision-making process from step one in order to come up with an effective solution. Ineffective decision-makers may just give up when something goes wrong or look for emotional relief rather than developing strategies to solve the problem. Recall the study noted earlier of small businesses devastated by a flood: those owners who immediately developed task-relevant coping strategies (e.g., to salvage what was left of the physical facilities, to get new financing, to continue to service customers, to keep their employees working) recovered much faster financially than those who spent their time just worrying.

Perhaps the single biggest enemy of effective decision-making is *emotion*.[11] Emotions are crucially important to every individual's health and happiness, but *they are not tools of knowledge*. The three emotions which most commonly undermine successful decision-making are fear (including anxiety and self-doubt), anger, and impatience. Because of fear or self-doubt, an individual may not want to face a difficult problem. Maybe he feels that he could not handle it, or that he would make a mistake, or that he would have to discard a pet preconception proven wrong, or that he would suffer embarrassment or pain. So the decision is avoided; meanwhile things just get worse.

Everyone has had the experience of jumping to a conclusion and angrily bawling out an employee, customer, or supplier, only to discover that one had misinterpreted the facts, or that one was not aware of some crucial fact, or that one could have found a better solution than the one chosen in anger. Similarly, everyone at some time has been faced with a decision that one wanted to get over with as fast as possible, only to regret it later. Hasty decisions are made on the basis of limited understanding of the issues and alternatives involved or on the basis of distorted judgments about what is important (e.g., hiring an employee because of one attribute, such as appearance or background, without considering other attributes).

There is a useful rule to follow when you feel impelled to set or implement a goal under the influence of a strong emotion: don't! Wait for the emotion to subside before taking any action.

The alternative to emotion in decision-making is *reason*. Reason is the faculty for identifying and evaluating facts objectively and for projecting the future. It is by means of reason that an effective decision-maker (1) accepts the challenge posed by a problem or potential problem; (2) considers a wide range of alternatives; (3) evaluates those alternatives against objective standards; (4) anticipates setbacks and makes contingency plans to deal with them; and (5) overcomes actual setbacks through a process of task centered problem-solving.

Besides learning how to make better decisions, another useful technique for reducing stress is to break complex and long-range goals down into simple short-range goals. For example, if a CEO's goal is to increase profitability, he or she should formulate a number of simpler, constituent goals (e.g., reduce costs, increase sales), each of which may in turn be divided into yet simpler goals (e.g., reduce costs by reducing turnover, raise productivity by eliminating re-work, etc.). Similarly, if the goal is to double the market penetration of a product within two years, set shorter term subgoals for each three or six month period during this time span. Or if a project has a deadline, set separate deadlines for each subphase of the project so that the overall deadline is met at the end. To put the issue more broadly, every big problem consists of a group of smaller problems; goal setting can and should be organized accordingly.

THE JOY OF STRESS

Thus far, we have been discussing the deleterious effects of stress. But this emphasis is somewhat misleading, for stress can be a positive factor both in work and in life. Much depends on how you view the obstacles to attaining your goals and values. If you see them as frightening, demeaning, or unfair, you may react with fear or anger, make poor decisions, feel unhappy in your work, and suffer psychological or physical symptoms. But if instead you see the obstacles as a challenge to be overcome, calling forth your greatest effort and the chance to use the full range of your skills and abilities, you can experience enormous excitement, a sense of purpose, and the pride and joy of accomplishment.

In this respect the lack of positive stress, in the sense of lack of challenge or the chance to grow, may actually be deleterious. For example, Professor Arthur Kornhauser, based on a study of work and mental health, claims that:

> The unsatisfactory mental health of working people consists in no small measure of their dwarfed desires and deadened initiative, reduction of their goals and restriction of their efforts to a point where life is relatively empty and only half meaningful. . . . if they want too little, the consequence is a drab existence devoid of color, exhilaration, and self-esteem.[12]

The need to set high goals if one wants to accomplish anything worthwhile is nicely expressed in the following quotation (of unknown origin): "People who have been successful in everything they have attempted have set their goals too low."

We have never seen anyone express the "joy of stress" better than the famed adventurer George Leigh Mallory, who described his motivation in attempting to scale Mt. Everest as follows:

> So, if you cannot understand that there is something in man which responds to the challenge of this mountain and goes out to meet it, that the struggle is the struggle of life itself upward and forever upward, then you won't see why we go. What we get from this adventure is just sheer joy. And joy is, after all, the end of life. We do not live to eat and make money. We eat and make money to be able to enjoy life. This is what life means and what life is for.[13]

SUMMARY

Stress occurs when an important goal or value is threatened, action is required to deal with the threat, there is uncertainty as to the outcome, and anxiety is experienced. Stress pertains to a relationship between the individual and the situation; individuals who chronically fail to use rational coping techniques are most easily threatened. Goal setting can entail stress when goals are difficult with risk of failure, or when there is goal overload, goal conflict, or goal ambiguity. Each of these sources of stress can be reduced or eliminated in a number of different ways. Goal setting can also reduce or prevent stress by making expectations clear and by promoting a sense of efficacy (when the goals are reached). The stress induced by complex goals can be mitigated by following the guidelines for effective decision-making and by breaking down complex goals into simpler ones. Stress should not be viewed solely as a negative influence; the challenge of overcoming obstacles can provide excitement and joy—it can be the fuel that impels men to great achievements.

9 • *Goal setting and other motivational techniques*

Goal setting is more than a technique that works. It is also a theory that helps to explain why other motivational techniques or approaches, some of which may seem at first glance to have little in common with goal setting, also work. Eight such approaches are discussed below.

SCIENTIFIC MANAGEMENT

The *scientific management* approach of Frederick W. Taylor[1] is typically associated with time and motion study and with the use of incentives. It is less commonly known that a key element of scientific management was the *task* concept. The task was a specific assignment involving a certain amount of work of a certain quality to be completed by an employee each day using specific tools and work motions. The task, in short, was a goal; time and motion study were used to specify the task. Incentives were paid as a reward for task accomplishment, but Taylor considered the task or goal to be the key motivational concept in his approach to management.

MANAGEMENT BY OBJECTIVES

Scientific management was the forerunner of *management by objectives*.[2] In the early 1900s Pierre Du Pont and Donaldson

107

Brown of the Du Pont Powder Company used Taylor's ideas on cost control and cost accounting to measure organizational and departmental performance. Later these ideas were institutionalized by Alfred P. Sloan at General Motors, where such performance measures were used to generate goals for managers.

While the *term* management by objectives was coined by Peter Drucker in the 1950s (based on his work at General Electric with Harold Smiddy), Sloan may have been the first to actually *use* this technique.[3] To repeat a quote cited earlier, Sloan anticipated the results of later goal setting research when he said that:

> The guiding principle was to make our standards difficult to achieve, but possible to attain, which I believe is the most effective way of capitalizing on the initiative, resourcefulness and capabilities of operating personnel.[4]

JOB ENRICHMENT

The importance of goal setting is less obvious in the technique of *job enrichment*, which was first popularized by Frederick Herzberg in the 1960s.[5] Herzberg's major argument was that many jobs failed to satisfy employee needs, specifically the need for psychological growth (e.g., learning, creativity, and so on), because the jobs they were doing were too repetitive and mentally unchallenging.

As an antidote to such deprivation, Herzberg urged that jobs be enriched through changes in their design. For example, he suggested that the level of responsibility in most jobs could be increased by giving people more discretion and autonomy in decision-making. This would involve, in effect, delegating some supervisory responsibilities to the employee. Herzberg also recommended that people be given a complete piece of work (or module) rather than an isolated part of it. Most importantly, he suggested that they be given direct *feedback* regarding the results of their work, especially with respect to quality. This feedback could come from the employee's personal inspection of the product, from another department which received the work product, or from an outside source such as a customer who used the product.

We have argued previously that feedback alone will not improve performance. However, it is almost impossible to consistently provide someone with feedback regarding work quality (or quantity) and not have him or her develop at least implicit standards regarding what constitutes "good" feedback and what constitutes "bad" feedback. It is a natural tendency, when one's work is measured, to want to know how good it is. But to determine this requires a standard against which the measurements can be judged.

Such implicit standards may come from various sources. For example, people may compare their scores informally with one another. Their supervisor's off-hand comments may indicate that what was achieved is adequate or requires further improvement. Customer comments may suggest that better performance is needed to please them.

Thus, in theory, any system that provides systematic feedback can foster goal setting *even when goals are not explicitly assigned* by management. After all, why would management even bother to develop a work measurement system to inform workers of their performance if it did not care about the outcome?

Studies of job enrichment have found that the most reliable performance outcome of this technique is an improvement in work quality.[6] Since most job enrichment studies involve quality feedback, it is probable that its motivational benefits are mainly due to feedback associated with goal setting. An experiment by Dr. Denis Umstot and his colleagues at the University of Washington supports this interpretation.[7] When they enriched a job while carefully eliminating all elements of goal setting, job enrichment did *not* lead to any improvement in productivity. Only when explicit goal setting was included did productivity increase.

It should be added that many changes introduced in the course of job enrichment programs are not directly motivational in nature, and yet they may have substantial benefits in and of themselves. For example, in many such programs, unnecessary tasks are eliminated, people are cross-trained on different jobs to increase flexibility, work flow and procedures are simplified, and tools and equipment are improved. Such changes can have substantial benefits on employee performance independent of their effects on an individual's motivation.

ORGANIZATIONAL BEHAVIOR MODIFICATION

The element of goal setting is more obvious in a technique that became popular in the 1970s, namely, *organizational behavior modification*. Proponents of this approach use terms such as "stimulus," "response," and "reinforcement" interchangeably with the words goal setting, feedback, and praise.

The actual procedures most commonly used by organizations that practice behavior modification include:

1. The specification of explicit standards of performance;
2. The provision of feedback showing the relation of performance to the standards; and
3. The presentation of a reward such as praise, recognition, or money for attaining the standards.

These procedures are indistinguishable from the basic procedures of goal setting.[8] Consider, for example, the work that was done at Emery Air Freight Co. The company wanted responses to customer queries within ninety minutes. After assigning this goal, the company asked operators to keep track of the time it took to reply to each call on a special checklist. From this information, the percentage of calls answered within the deadline was calculated. Employees were praised whenever they attained their daily objective, which was to answer 90 percent to 95 percent of the calls within the deadline. Not surprisingly, the result was a rapid and substantial improvement in performance.

PARTICIPATION

Goal setting has long been associated with the technique of participative management. *Participation* has been recommended by many behavioral scientists since the 1930s as a powerful motivational technique.

In many organizational settings where participation studies were conducted, goal setting was an integral part of participation—for example, employees were asked for their opinions on where the goal or standard should be set. The results were often successful in terms of increasing productivity, but these studies did not answer a basic question: was it the participation, the goal setting, or both that brought about the increase?

As noted in Chapter 5, the answer is that it was goal setting. Participation in *setting* goals, although it may help, is not mandatory for goal setting to be effective.[9] Assigned goals seem to work as well as goals set jointly by the manager and subordinate; most employees will accept assigned goals providing they are seen as fair and reasonable.

Participation, on the other hand, may be very beneficial as a means of *implementing* goals, e.g., developing suitable action plans. The most successful study of participation to date involved hospital laundry workers who suggested ways to improve the efficiency of their unit. When their suggestions were implemented, productivity rose more than 50 percent![10] The benefits with respect to implementation are, of course, cognitive rather than motivational because they are a result of better ideas rather than more effort on the part of the employees. Motivation, however, may be involved indirectly. Employees will not bother to make suggestions if their ideas, regardless of their merit, are consistently ignored.

SYSTEM 4

Some readers may be familiar with *System 4*, the managerial philosophy put forth by Rensis Likert of the University of Michigan.[11] Key elements of System 4 include:

1. Participation in decision-making at all levels of the organization, including downward, upward, diagonal, and horizontal communication;
2. Structural features such as group tasks and overlapping work groups that foster such communication and participation; and
3. Commitment to high goals by all members of the organization.

Observe that goal setting is a key component of System 4. Dr. Likert argued that participation is essential to ensure goal acceptance. However, as noted earlier, substantial numbers of experiments conducted in various organizations show that participation is not essential in order for goals to be accepted. Rather what may be essential is *supportiveness* on the part of the supervisor (see Chapter 5). A supportive supervisor makes sure that the employee clearly understands the goal, and helps and encourages the employee who has difficulty reaching the goal, rather than invoking punishment.

COMPETITION

Competition is another technique in which goal setting plays a key role. In fact, *competition is a special form of goal setting in which the performance of some other person serves as the goal.* Competition can be an extraordinary motivator for two reasons. First, in competition the goal gets more and more difficult over time as the losers strive to improve enough to become winners. Second, some people find it more satisfying to beat another person than to beat an impersonal standard. Another person's performance is for them more meaningful than a standard that is not based on any particular person's performance; beating a person who is trying to win feels like a greater achievement than beating an impersonal standard that just "sits there." (Formal competition, as noted in Chapter 5, should be used with great caution because it entails definite risks, for example, apathy on the part of chronic losers or greater focus on beating the other person than on the goals of the organization).

MONETARY INCENTIVES

The most fundamental connection between money and goal setting is that *paying employees for their services makes them willing to expend time and effort on the organization's behalf.* Given this willingness to expend effort, goals tell the employee *where* to expend the effort (direction); *how much* to exert it (effort and persistence); and *how* to exert it (work strategy).

Monetary incentive plans are often associated with either explicit or implicit goals. The reason is that payment must be dependent on the achievement of *something.* In the case of the classic one-tiered piece-rate plan, whereby the individual is paid a certain amount for each piece produced or paid a commission for each unit sold, payment is not tied to goal attainment. However, most such plans have minimum productivity standards based on time study or past experience, which the employees are expected to meet.[12] And even if there are no standards, the employees often set their own goals, both as a method of creating additional interest in the job and as a way of translating their desired earnings goals into performance terms. If they do not, the piece-rate system has a minimal effect on productivity.

An interesting variant on the traditional piece-rate system was introduced in the mid-1970s among unionized mountain beaver trappers who worked for a forest products company in the northwest. The employees were guaranteed their usual hourly pay but in addition were paid a bonus based on the number of mountain beavers actually trapped. Half the trappers were paid a $1 bonus for each mountain beaver; the other half were paid a $4 bonus contingent on trapping a beaver and correctly guessing the color of a marble they were to draw out of a paper bag. Since there were four different marbles of known colors, they could earn $1 per beaver on the average. The gambling aspect of the payoff system was found to add an element of excitement to the job, which the trappers found highly rewarding. Overall costs were reduced 23 percent per beaver for both groups despite the bonus system, and productivity increased 41 percent.[13] One of the consequences of introducing this incentive system was that many trappers spontaneously set goals for themselves. Those who did so tended to increase their productivity more than those who did not.[14]

All levels of employees from the shop floor to the top executive can benefit from the explicit tie between goals and money under individual task and bonus plans. The individual is paid for meeting or exceeding an individual goal. There are many variations on this basic idea. For example, at the turn of the century Frederick W. Taylor developed a "differential piece-rate" plan in which an employee was paid at a low rate if he produced less than the assigned task and at a substantially higher rate if he reached the task assigned to him. On this score it is worth recalling the findings reported in Chapter 3 (see Figure 2, p. 24) that people with very hard goals under a task and bonus scheme may give up if partial success is not rewarded at all and total success (attaining the task) seems impossible.

Two group versions of the task and bonus concept include the Scanlon Plan, a plant-wide incentive scheme where the employees' bonus depends on beating a certain historically based ratio of payroll costs to the value of production. Under Mitchell Fein's Improshare Plan, employees receive a bonus depending on the man hours required to achieve a given amount and type of production as compared with the corresponding man hours required before the plan went into effect.[15] The monetary gains from improvement in speed are shared 50/50 between workers and management.

As noted earlier, there is a certain risk in paying people for goal success. To the degree that they have influence over what goals are set, they may be motivated to set easy goals in order to be sure of reaching them. There are several ways around this. First, goals can be assigned by those at a higher level so that the employee has no say as to the level of the goal. Second, as noted in Chapter 4, all goals can be rated as to difficulty, and people can be paid as a function of both the difficulty of the goal and the degree of goal accomplishment. Third, employees can participate in developing their own pay plans. In the few places where this has been tried, employees have been found to be highly conscientious and have developed plans that have been viewed by both employees and management as fair.

Another alternative is to widen the gap between goal achievement and pay. Goals can simply be used as guidelines, and payment (raises, performance evaluations) can be based on performance rather than on goal attainment as such. Thus an individual who set high goals but did not reach them could still get a higher rating than one who successfully attained easy goals because the former's actual performance was higher. On the one hand, this method is less objective since allocation of rewards must be left to the discretion of those with the relevant authority. However, a possible benefit of this approach is that the punitive aspect of failure (in terms of lost rewards) is reduced.

To illustrate the enormous combined power of goals and incentives, consider the experience of Nucor Corporation, one of the fastest growing and most profitable mini-mill steel companies in the United States. It sells specialty steel products at a price well below the price of steel imported from any country. President Ken Iverson says: "We only do two things well: build plants economically and run them very efficiently with high productivity."[16] Their nonunion production workers are given a relatively low base pay but can earn an additional bonus of 100 percent to 200 percent based on the amount of steel they produce. The result: it takes Nucor 20 percent fewer man hours to make a ton of steel than the Japanese and 50 percent fewer man hours than many competing U.S. mills. Managers are also on an incentive system based on the company's return on equity.

We noted in an earlier chapter that monetary incentives can facilitate goal commitment. It is now worth considering times when actual payment for goal success is necessary or advisable.

To start, it should be noted that even in cases where there is no explicit tie between goal attainment and money, there is still an implicit tie as long as the organization uses a merit system for raises and promotions. In such a case, good performance will still be rewarded in the long run.

We believe that monetary bonuses for goal success are most useful and necessary when:

1. The employee is being asked to show a substantial increase in performance that necessitates *working substantially harder than in the past.* Such a situation might arise where there is a strong union shop and a history of substantial featherbedding and restriction of output. Union–management relations may also show a history of continual antagonism and conflict. In such a case it may take a big payoff to break out of the rut. Fein's Improshare Plan, as well as the Scanlon Plan, were developed specifically to foster labor–management cooperation. In the Fein plan, employees and management split 50/50 on any bonus obtained as a result of increased production. As a result, both benefit equally from cooperating to improve efficiency, so long as no layoffs occur as a result of increased production. In contrast, if the issue is simply a change in work methods or strategy, for example, working smarter rather than harder, direct incentive payments for goal accomplishment may be unnecessary. In addition, as we shall see in Chapter 10, unions themselves may be opposed to incentive pay even when they approve of goal setting itself, perhaps out of fear that the incentives will be used as a tool of punishment.

2. *The job requires an unusual degree of initiative,* as in selling, so that a good deal of inertia and fear of failure must be overcome in order to motivate a high level of productive activity.

3. *The employees take little pleasure in achievement* for its own sake and view their jobs solely as a means of earning a living. This is most likely to be the case with unskilled and semi-skilled jobs where many incumbents have limited abilities and limited ambitions.

Several years ago we examined all the available experiments that have reported the effect on performance of one or more motivational techniques.[17] We grouped these studies, more than sixty in all, into four basic categories: money, goal setting, participation, and job enrichment. The studies of monetary incentives were in turn divided into group and individual plans. For each study, we calculated the average improvement in performance (quantity, quality, sales, etc.) obtained as a result of introducing the techniques in question. The results for each technique are shown below.

MOTIVATION TECHNIQUE	MEDIAN IMPROVEMENT IN PERFORMANCE
Money, individual incentives	30%
Money, group incentives	20%
Goal setting	16%
Job enrichment	9%
Participation	0.5%

Clearly these findings are very promising in terms of the potential for money to improve performance, and they are clearly consistent with the argument that money can raise the motivation level of employees to the extent that it results in the individual setting and/or accepting specific challenging goals.

As indicated by the above results, there are two basic types of incentive plans: individual and group. Each type has at least one major advantage and one potential drawback.

Individual plans reward each individual according to his or her own performance, and thus the connection between performance and reward is very strong. However, such plans do not typically reward individuals for cooperation; helping other employees could even detract from one's own performance.

Group plans are exactly the opposite; they reward individual effort less reliably, since payment is divided among any number of individuals. On the other hand, cooperation is far more likely to be rewarded since payment is based on the total group output.

The choice between these two types of plans must depend on such factors as the nature of the work tasks (the degree of cooperation required), the preferences of the employees, the ease of measuring individual and group output, and the stability of task assignments.

Incentive plans require certain conditions before they will be effective.[18] These guidelines include the following:

1. The employees must value the extra money they will make under the plan. This can be insured in at least two ways: by selecting employees who want to increase their earning power, and by making the potential bonuses large enough to be psychologically and economically meaningful to them. During selection, employees can be asked whether they would value working according to a system whereby they are paid according to the quantity and/or quality of their own (or a group's) performance. Both prospective and existing employees can be asked how much additional money they would have to earn over and above their normal hourly or weekly pay in order to make extra effort worthwhile. Our guess is that employees usually will respond favorably if they can increase their earnings by at least 5 percent to 10 percent. Most find the opportunity to make 10 percent to 20 percent more money to be highly motivating.

Incentive plans must always be used with caution, however, because they sometimes backfire. For example, employees with modest income aspirations might use the extra money to take a day off rather than to earn more money. Thus, they might prefer the same pay as before for four days work rather than 25 percent more pay for five days work. This problem may not be very likely to occur in Western countries beset by inflation, but it has been reported many times when Western companies introduced incentives into factories in less-developed societies where the workers were content with modest earnings.

2. The employees must not lose important values as a result of high performance. Most importantly there must be no rate cutting and there should be no layoffs. No intelligent employee will work hard today if the result will be more work tomorrow just to keep the same pay. Nor will most employees work hard knowing they will work themselves out of a job. Rate cutting can be prevented by having a company policy (that is actually followed!) against it and, in addition, by studying jobs very carefully before introducing incentives so that earnings on one or more jobs do not get way out of line.

In addition, special devices have been developed to protect the employee against losses caused by rate cutting. Under

Mitchell Fein's Improshare Plan (described earlier), if employees improve their speed by a very large amount, e.g., more than 60 percent, the excess money goes into a special fund and this fund is used to "buy back" the man-hour standard from the employees at the end of the year. In other words, the employees each are paid a lump sum in return for allowing management to raise the hourly standard.

Most employees prefer making less money to endangering their health or safety. It may also be the case that some employees will restrict output for strictly social-psychological reasons, e.g., to enhance group solidarity through de-emphasizing competition. But, as noted earlier, the ultimate motivator for restriction of output is often economic. The group may believe that high output will be detrimental to them in some way. In those cases where restriction is motivated strictly by social motives, it might be overcome by substituting group for individual incentives.

3. Employees must be able to control their performance. In other words, they must have some influence over the quantity or quality of goods produced, or the time taken to do the job, or the amount of sales or profits, or the like.

Consider an extreme case, for example, in which a manager has a sales goal but a crucial flaw is discovered in the product, and no more units can be sold for six months until the problem is corrected. It would be ludicrous to expect the sales force to be motivated to sell a product that is not yet available. Or to use a real life example, the federal government not long ago required certain officials to attain specific EEO hiring goals (i.e., minority quotas) as a condition for receiving a bonus and then placed a freeze on hiring!

Especially in the case of managerial jobs, determining what the manager can control and cannot control may be a very complex matter. Consider, for example, the manager of a bank branch or of a fast food restaurant. The major factors affecting bank deposits on the one hand and food sales on the other will be such matters as location, product quality, price, type of service, and hours. All of these are typically determined by the central office and therefore are not controllable by the branch manager. Thus basing incentive payments on deposits or sales would be both useless and unfair. Such performance measures would properly be replaced by other more appropriate measures, e.g., customer service, cleanliness, etc.

Another aspect of this problem is employee ability. Employees cannot increase their performance if they do not have the requisite aptitude or knowledge. There are only two ways to insure adequate ability: proper selection and adequate training and/or experience.

4. The employees must clearly understand how the plan works. Some incentive plans are so complicated that the employees cannot figure out exactly how their increased effort translates into more money. As a result they become apathetic toward the program.

At a recent conference, the president of a small company related how he successfully introduced Fein's Improshare Plan into his company. Productivity improved dramatically but then began to tail off. The top officials of the company met with the employees to ask them what was causing the drop in production. It turned out that the production employees had forgotten how the plan worked! After some additional educational sessions, production soared once again.

The implication is clear: keep the plan simple and explain it clearly as many times as is necessary to insure complete understanding by the employees.

5. It must be possible to measure performance accurately. In Chapter 3 we discussed two basic ways that performance could be measured: through direct measurement of output (e.g., production, sales, etc.) and through the use of Behavioral Observation Scales, which measure the frequency with which each of a number of actions is taken.

If performance is not, or for some reason cannot, be measured accurately, it will be very difficult to set up an incentive plan that will be accepted by the employees, since there will be endless complaints and disagreements about who should get what and how much.

Some incentive schemes run into problems because they reward an individual only for a small but easily measured part rather than for all phases of the job. As a result, the individual may spend most of his or her efforts on that aspect of the job and neglect other important but unrewarded aspects. If an incentive plan is to be maximally effective, the performance measure on which the rewards are based must be comprehensive.

An oil company once asked us to determine why their salespeople were pushing one product at the expense of several others despite repeated verbal and written orders from their supervisors to push the other products equally hard. The diagnosis was made within seconds. We asked if a monetary incentive was paid for selling the product that was pushed the hardest. The answer was yes. In contrast, all that the salespersons received for selling the other products was a pat on the back.

If a Behavioral Observation Scale is used, it is important that the employees trust those making the observations and ratings. To prevent poor sampling and bias on the part of observers, ratings about a given individual should be obtained from several sources, such as peers, subordinates, and supervisors or managers (as noted in Chapter 7).

SUMMARY

Goal setting plays a role in the success of many motivational techniques, including scientific management, MBO, job enrichment, organizational behavior modification, participation, System 4, competition, and monetary incentives. Thus, goal setting is more than just a motivational technique; *it is a core motivational technique,* one on which many others depend or work through.[19] Any given motivational technique will be effective to the degree that it generates or is associated with the setting of specific, challenging goals and/or the degree to which it enhances commitment to those goals.

Money is a fundamental motivator because of its role as a medium of exchange; it enables people to help fulfill both physical and psychological needs and attain their life goals.

Goals can be linked to monetary payoffs in several ways, e.g., piece-rates, task and bonus systems, scores on Behavioral Observation Scales, and historical ratios. Studies have shown that incentive plans raise performance, on the average, between 20 percent and 30 percent. Individual plans may be more useful when the jobs are independent; group plans may work better when substantial cooperation is needed among organization members. To work effectively, incentive plans must ensure that the extra pay is valued; no important values are lost; the employees can control their performance; the employees understand how the plan works; and performance can be measured reasonably accurately.

10 • *Goal setting with unionized workers*

As we have stressed throughout this book, one of the most replicable findings in the motivational literature is that the setting of specific, difficult goals leads to increases in productivity. Goal setting studies, however, have generally been conducted with nonunionized workers. Unions have generally been concerned primarily with issues such as pay, job security, and, in some instances, the quality of work life. Union hierarchies have typically shunned the endorsement of policies or procedures that explicitly focus on productivity improvement.

One study, mentioned briefly in Chapters 1 and 2, that did focus on goal setting with unionized employees was conducted in the mid-1970s.[1] Unionized drivers in the southwestern United States were not loading their trucks to capacity. Instead, the trucks were being loaded to only 60 percent of the maximum legal load possible. Attaching scales to the trucks was not feasible from a cost/benefit standpoint because the trucks were driven constantly over rough terrain, causing the scales to break.

Exhorting the drivers for three consecutive months to try harder than they had in the past resulted in no increase in productivity. As a last resort, the company approached the union with a goal setting program.

The company explained the productivity problem to the union, emphasizing that no one would be rewarded with monetary bonuses for attaining the goal, a policy which the union endorsed. Similarly, it was stressed that no one would be punished for failing to attain the goal. With this understanding, a specific goal of 94 percent of maximum allowable truck weight was agreed upon by the company and the union as a reasonable one to assign to the drivers.

The union in this case showed relatively little interest in the program once it was agreed that there would be no penalties for ignoring the goal. The union felt that employees would simply ignore the goals if goal attainment were voluntary!

Measures of the net weight of all thirty-six truck drivers were collected for three consecutive months prior to the introduction of goal setting. In order to be certain that fluctuations in weather and season would not bias the results favorably, these pre-measures were collected when working conditions were optimal, that is, during July, August, and September. The results of the goal setting were monitored for nine consecutive months following the start of the goal setting program, that is, October through June.

The results are shown in Figure 5. It is evident that setting a specific, difficult goal led to a substantial increase in performance. Moreover, it is evident that this increase held up across time despite changes in season (fall, winter, and spring).

Interviews with the drivers concerning the temporary drop in performance during the second month of the goal setting program revealed that they were testing management's statement that no punitive steps would be taken against them if performance suddenly dropped. No such steps were taken and performance again increased.

Without the increase in efficiency due to goal setting, the company would have spent a quarter of a million dollars to buy additional trucks to deliver the same quantity of materials. This figure does not include the cost of additional diesel fuel that would have been consumed or the expense of recruiting, hiring, and training additional truck drivers. The effects of the goals have endured to this day, more than eight years later!

It might be argued that it was not goal setting but feedback to the drivers regarding their truck's weight that caused the dramatic increase in their performance. This explanation can

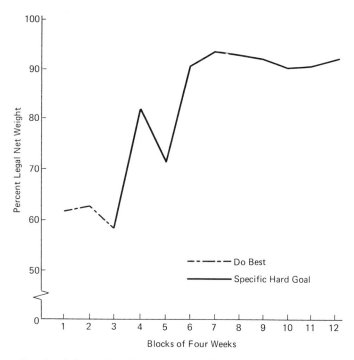

SOURCE: Reprinted from G. Latham and J. Baldes, "The 'Practical Significance' of Locke's Theory of Goal Setting," *Journal of Applied Psychology*, 1975, Vol. 60, 123. Copyright, 1975, by the American Psychological Association.

Figure 5 • Truck Driver Performance

be ruled out, however, because the truck's weight had always been available to each driver as soon as the truck was weighed in the truck yard.

The present findings support the thesis that feedback or knowledge of results does not affect one's motivation to perform unless it is used to set (or track) a specific, hard goal. However, it was interesting to note that subsequent to goal setting the drivers voluntarily began to record their truck weight on a trip sheet. Thus, goal setting increased the salience or importance of feedback (their truck weight) to them. The feedback revealed progress in relation to the goal and also fostered a feeling of success and pride when it signified goal accomplishment.

Similarly, the notion that the improvement in performance was due solely to competition (a type of goal setting!) among the drivers, rather than individual goal setting, was rejected because no special prizes or formal recognition programs were provided for those people who came closest to or exceeded the goal. No winner or winners were singled out by the company. Furthermore, the opportunity for competition to occur prior to goal setting had always existed for the drivers through their knowledge of the daily and weekly truck weights of each of the other drivers. However, interviews with and observations of the drivers indicated that goal setting did lead to informal competition among them. This competition may help explain why the drivers have remained committed to this challenging goal to the present day.

Finally, the suggestion that the improvement in performance could have been due to the pervasive Hawthorne Effect (i.e., the effects of attention itself) was ruled out because the amount of attention provided for the drivers was the same prior to and during the goal setting process. The only additional instruction given to the supervisors was to praise drivers who met or exceeded the goal and to withhold negative comments when the goal was not met. The supervisors tried to follow these instructions, although they did not always do it consistently.

Why was goal setting so effective? The answers have been discussed throughout this book. In this particular instance, we found that the setting of a goal that is both specific and challenging made it clear to the drivers what was required of them. This in turn provided them with a sense of achievement, recognition, and commitment in that the drivers could compare present performance with how well they had done in the past, and in some instances with how well they were doing in comparison to others. Thus these employees were not only encouraged to expend more carefully directed effort, but they devised better or more creative tactics for ensuring that these efforts would succeed. On their own initiative, several drivers made recommendations for minor modifications of their trucks. These modifications included raising the forward stakes in the truck, which, in some cases, enabled the drivers to increase the accuracy of their judgments as to the weight of the load they were carrying.

In summary, it is evident that goal setting can be effective among unionized workers. An issue that remains to be addressed is how to gain union cooperation for goal setting. In the above study, the union was rather indifferent to goal setting, but this is frequently not the case.

APPROACHING RECALCITRANT UNIONS ABOUT GOAL SETTING

Getting union support for goal setting can be a difficult undertaking. If goal setting is viewed by the rank and file as a means of making them work harder than they already are, or as a gimmick solely for improving productivity at the workers' expense, then union support for the goal setting could lead to the ouster of union officials and their replacement by individuals whose beliefs reflect those of the membership.

With these issues in mind, we approached a union to develop guidelines on ways of attaining their support for goal setting.[2] The union business agents were interviewed in the union hall.

Before asking for their cooperation, the potential benefit of goal setting for employees was explained in terms of encouraging pride, efficacy, excitement, interest, and so on. Because the business agents had performed the job in question, they had no difficulty recognizing that goal setting could turn the most routine, repetitive task (like golf or bowling) into a challenging game.

In addition, the necessity for improving productivity was discussed. No attempt was made to hide this purpose from them. Finally, the union officials were asked to specify the conditions under which they would support goal setting.

The business agents specified five conditions as necessary

for them to accept goal setting for the purpose of increasing productivity without the requirement of formal negotiations with the union.

1. Working to attain the assigned goal must be *voluntary* for an employee.
2. There must be *no monetary rewards* for or special treatment of those people who attain the goal. The union contract prohibited the use of monetary incentives for individual efforts.
3. *Supportive supervisory behavior*, i.e., setting a difficult but attainable goal for an employee, is encouraged provided that it is clear to the employee that working to attain the goal was voluntary. Verbal praise for goal attainment is acceptable supervisory behavior and does not constitute "special treatment" of employees. This is the kind of supportive behavior that the union would like to see all supervisors engage in whenever an employee does good work.
4. There must be *no punishment for failing* to attain a goal.
5. Most importantly, there must be *sufficient long-term work* so that goal attainment will not lead to layoffs or a reduction in the work force through attrition (i.e., a policy of not replacing an employee who leaves the company).

Upon receiving this information, a wood products company decided to implement a goal setting study with strict adherence to these five points.

IMPLEMENTING THE UNION GUIDELINES

After agreeing to these guidelines, a goal setting study was conducted with seventy-four unionized logging truck drivers. Thirty-nine drivers participated in the experimental group; thirty-five drivers formed the comparison group. All the truck drivers were male and each had worked for the company four or more years.

Prior to conducting this study, the drivers were often not at the logging sites when they were needed. Logs were stacked at the landing, ready to be transported, with no room to place additional logs. This held up the work flow. Supervision of the truck drivers was relatively lax, because only one truck foreman was in charge of each group of thirty-five to forty drivers. The foremen worked at a central location and were usually able to communicate with the truck drivers only by radio. However, since the truck drivers spent much of their time on the road and were not always accessible even by radio, they could not be directly supervised.

The drivers' explanations for their inefficiencies ranged from mild apathy to acknowledging outright violations of company rules. For example, it was not uncommon for drivers to admit to us that they frequently pulled off the road to talk to one another or to take an extended lunch hour. Since all the drivers had received intensive driver's training and orientation to company policy, additional training was not believed to be necessary for increasing their productivity. Economic conditions made it impossible to even consider the benefits, if any, of increasing the number of supervisors. It was for these reasons that the company decided that a motivation program for the truck drivers had to be developed.

Each Friday the truck foreman had always identified the logging sites that would be in operation the following week and the number of drivers that would be needed. With the implementation of the goal setting program, the foreman of the thirty-nine truck drivers in the experimental group introduced a weekly goal for each driver in terms of average number of trips per day from the logging sites to the mill. The goal took into account factors such as: (1) distance of the logging sites from the mill, (2) road conditions, (3) size of timber being logged, and (4) skill of the driver. The weekly goals ranged from an average of three to seven trips per truck per day.

When explaining the program to the truck drivers, the truck foreman stated that the goals were not "production standards," nor would any negative consequences occur if they were not met; rather, the goals were merely something for the drivers to strive for if they so desired. The importance of goal setting for injecting challenge into a task was stressed. The company also explained that the union had been informed of the program.

Subsequent to informing the drivers of the goal setting program, the weekly goal for each truck driver was written next to each driver's name and posted on a bulletin board in the room where they met each morning and evening with the truck foreman. An average weekly goal for the truck drivers as a group was also calculated and placed at the top of this sheet.

Each evening the foreman posted the information he received from the mill regarding the number of trips made by each truck driver. This information had always been collected by the foreman, but in the past it had been used only for his own recordkeeping purposes. This information had also always been available to an individual driver regarding his performance; for every load of logs taken in, each driver received a ticket receipt which he was free to keep for his own records.

We obtained trips-per-truck data for five weeks prior to the implementation of the goal setting program and for eighteen weeks after its implementation. In addition, data on trips per truck were obtained for the same time period on thirty-five drivers from another logging area for comparison purposes. This area was located in the same region as that where the goal setting program took place; it had a similar terrain and log mix; it had the same number of logging sites and approximately the same number of truck drivers; and it had similar production figures on trips-per-truck averages during the five week premeasure period as did the area where the goal setting program was implemented.

There was no appreciable difference in the performance of those who would be assigned goals (average = 3.55 trips) and those who would not (average = 3.49 trips) during the premeasure period. However, there was a substantial difference between the two groups following the implementation of the goal setting, with the goal setting group having a 22 percent greater average number of trips each day per truck (4.08) than the comparison group (3.34).

The average increase for the experimental group was .53

trips per day, while the performance of the comparison group actually declined slightly. Computed on a daily basis for the thirty-nine drivers over the eighteen-week goal setting period, the increase in number of truck trips was approximately 1,800. The value of the timber from one truck trip is approximately $1,500. Thus, the annual value of the increase in trips per truck of the goal setting group could be estimated at $2.7 million!

A potential flaw in drawing firm conclusions from this study is that it did not incorporate a true experimental design in the sense that the drivers were not randomly assigned to conditions. Thus it might be claimed that alternative explanations (e.g., workload requirements, technological differences, worker experience, work site differences) could account for the differences obtained between the goal setting and nongoal setting groups. However, the weight of the evidence indicates that it was goal setting that increased productivity.

One source of evidence is the similarity of the two geographical areas compared in this study. As previously stated, these two areas were extremely similar on a number of variables including the pre-measures of productivity. In fact, the superintendents of these two areas are compared quarterly on measures of productivity by upper management because of the similarities between the company's two logging districts. In the course of the study, the group that set goals achieved the highest weekly average number of trips per truck that had ever been obtained.

The hypothesis that differences in productivity between the two groups were due to employee experience or equipment was also rejected. The experience of the drivers and the age and type of equipment was approximately the same for both groups.

Also in favor of the goal setting explanation was the observation that the truck drivers were extremely aware of their goals. They were overheard repeatedly bragging about goal attainment as they came in for the evening. Several drivers who met their goals for the week purchased gold stars on their own and placed them beside their respective names. And, during a two-day holiday week that the truck foreman decided was too short to set goals, several annoyed drivers marched into his office and demanded that goals be set!

It was also observed that following the goal setting implementation, the truck drivers started doing several things differently, which raised their productivity. For example, the foreman reported that the drivers started to use their radios to coordinate their efforts so that there would always be a truck at the logging sites when timber was ready to be loaded. Thus goal setting led to the spontaneous development of action plans for improving performance.

VIOLATING THE GUIDELINES

Support for the validity of the union's guidelines was obtained through the following incident. The study on the effects of goal setting lasted eighteen weeks. During the nineteenth week the company hired a consulting firm specializing in time study to implement a formal goal setting program for all woods operations.

When the consulting firm began its work, the union employees were not told that the goals to be recommended by the consultants would be voluntary. The employees observed the consultants on the job site with stop watches. Rumor led them to believe that they would be required by the company to reach specific goals.

The employees believed that attainment of a goal would be tied to rewards and punishments. Many said that they thought they would be "browbeaten" for not attaining a goal. They also concluded that their jobs would be at stake if they did not attain the goals. The immediate consequence of this perception was a wildcat strike that lasted three days.

In order to make it clear to the union that the company would abide by the five points discussed earlier, the timberlands manager went to the union hall and explained that the goals set would be *voluntary*, as they had been in the past for the truck drivers. More importantly, he stressed that supervisors would be supportive of effective performance and goal attainment, but no negative comments or consequences would occur if goals were not met. He also emphasized that there would be no cutbacks or layoffs as a result of productivity increases.

After clarifying these issues, the manager asked the union members to give the program a two-month trial period after which they could reject the program if they were not satisfied with the way it was being run. The union agreed to these conditions.

Following this meeting, the manager met with all logging foremen. He emphasized the importance of adhering to the above points, and he stressed that their behavior toward the employees was critical to this program's success. The program is now in operation with no subsequent negative incidents or complaints.

Since we have described only two studies with unionized workers, we cannot guarantee that experiences like those above are representative of what others may experience with setting goals with unionized workers. However, it should be noted that the types of concerns voiced by the union involved in the above studies are quite typical of the concerns voiced by most unions. Observe especially the need for trust in management and what happens when that trust appears to have been violated.

In addition, it should be noted that the company involved in the above studies is not known for having especially cordial union–management relationships, although this union is not as militant as unions in some other industries. Our results show at least that union–management relations do not have to be outstanding for goal setting to be accepted—providing that mutually agreed on guidelines are followed.

TEAMBUILDING BETWEEN UNION AND MANAGEMENT

The present timing for mutual goal setting between management and labor in many industries is excellent. Labor unions are confronted with a loss of jobs by their members; management is confronted with escalating costs; both management and labor are confronted by a shrinking market. Thus both management and labor have a reason for becoming a team in order to set and attain jointly agreed on goals.

As noted in Chapters 4 and 7, goal setting is not restricted to outcome variables such as a given number of units to be produced within a specified time limit. Often it is as important, if not more important, to look at process variables, namely, behavior and/or perceptions of behavior as opposed to units produced per employee hour. This was the case with two companies and two union locals in the Pacific Northwest. The following is an integration of our experiences in these two cases.[3]

Management, in some instances, looked for ways of circumventing the labor contract. The union, in some instances, encouraged members to *look for* grievances to file. The result was constant work slowdowns, third-step grievance meetings, and strikes.

Top management in these two companies began to recognize the importance of using their human resources as one approach to improving productivy. This was a significant shift in strategy from the past thirty years when the emphasis was primarily on finding ways to mechanize operations in order to minimize a reliance on the labor force. They concluded that the development of the human resource could be straightforward if it included the setting of mutually agreed on goals with their respective unions. To do this, a teambuilding strategy was followed.

Teambuilding, as noted in previous chapters, is simply another way of saying that a team is formed whenever people can agree on (a) common concerns or objectives, (b) solutions to reach the objectives, and (c) who should do what and when to implement the solutions. The process of forming a team is similar, if not identical, in many respects to marital counseling. The two parties, management and labor, decide that "divorce" is not a viable alternative, and improving the "marriage" is of maximum benefit for both of them. Thus, a neutral party is sought who can provide an in-depth conflict resolution process that will allow them to build or rebuild a working relationship. The underlying structure to this process is *simplicity*.

For example, once management and labor had agreed on the need for teambuilding, two simple ground rules were established. First, all discussions were restricted to how management and labor could improve their contract. Nothing was said or done to circumvent the collective bargaining process. Furthermore, it was agreed that teambuilding was not to be an extension of or substitution for a standing committee meeting. Grievances were not to be discussed. This led to agreement on a second rule. All discussions must emphasize the future: "What specifically are we going to do differently?" The reason for this rule was that one person's memory and perception of an event might have differed from that of another person; the past cannot be undone, so there was little benefit in discussing it.

In selecting the people who would attempt to form a team, management selected a manager, a superintendent, and several key first-line supervisors. The president and the business agent of the union local, in addition to themselves, selected the shop stewards, heads of various committees (e.g., safety), and people who had expressed a strong interest in the process to them. The total number of people usually varied from eight to twenty.

Teambuilding interviews. Each person was interviewed by a neutral party and was assured of confidentiality. The neutral party was an industrial psychologist knowledgeable in group processes and conflict resolution and was viewed as truly neutral by both management and the union. Each person was asked the same questions. The questions were simple and direct:

> 1. What is management/union doing right in their relationship with one another? The purpose of this question was to allow both parties to see how far they had to go in establishing a working relationship. Both sides were pleased to see that, collectively, there was much that was perceived favorably by them. Examples of responses given to this inquiry by management regarding the union include:
>> a. Most of them do not seek out problems.
>> b. They're well informed on safety.

c. The standing committee knows the contract; they are more knowledgeable than we are.

d. When the union local has a bona fide problem, they give management the opportunity to gather the facts to respond to it before getting everyone aroused.

Examples of responses given to this inquiry by the union regarding management include:

a. If there is a difference in opinion in interpreting contract language, they are now beginning to explain their interpretations to us so it doesn't appear that they are just trying to pull a fast one on us.

b. They really put the money into the safety program. The foremen are right there to point out and solve safety issues.

c. The foremen are good. They know their jobs, which enables them to get us to do our work properly.

d. The supervisors are beginning to compliment us for a job well done.

2. What would you like to see management/union start doing, stop doing, or do differently? The answers to this question formed the basis for setting specific goals. Examples of answers given to this question by management include:

a. We need to get a workable understanding of posting with the union. A person shouldn't be allowed to change jobs every month.

b. We need a workable understanding of what it means to select the most senior *qualified* individual. Competency must be stressed along with seniority.

c. We need open discussion on a potential grievance prior to writing it out. When an employee has a problem, the person should talk first to the supervisor. Saying "I'm going to file a grievance" is not talking it out. The correct procedure is to talk the issue out with the supervisor, then to go to the superintendent if the issue is not resolved, and then to file a grievance if the issue is still not resolved.

Examples of answers to this question given by the union include:

a. Tell us in advance of things that are brewing. In this way we can head things off before a grievance is filed. Once a grievance is filed, things become set as to what both sides have to do. Before the grievance is filed there's a chance to be creative.

b. More needs to be done by management on recordkeeping: who is working, who is laid off and when, when is that person coming back, etc.

c. Get cooperation among the units within a department. The competition among units is absurd.

d. We file grievances because your word isn't worth anything. We have to document through grievances. Honor your word, improve your memory, and many grievances will be eliminated.

3. What can you (management/union) do to improve the working relationship? This question was asked to see to what extent the parties from the outset were truly interested in taking the first step in working together. Representative comments from management include:

a. We need to build trust through frankness/openness with them. We're not devious now, but we don't always remember to tell them everything about bumping rights/ responsibilities.

b. We need to communicate the *why's* behind unpopular decisions.

c. We need to meet the requirements of the contract in spirit as well as to the letter. We need to truly know and understand the contract.

d. We need to make an all-out effort to get rid of perceptions of favoritism and inconsistency.

The union's responses included:

a. Stop patting ourselves on the back for "got you" feelings. Realize we too are here to make a profit for the company or there won't be any jobs for our people.

b. Get with the company and help them on seniority/ bumping call backs. Stop trying to "catch them."

c. Be tactful in dealing with supervisors; be less brassy.

d. Keep communication lines open rather than plotting and scheming.

THE TEAMBUILDING MEETING

After the interviews were conducted, a neutral party or facilitator edited the comments and grouped them together in terms of underlying themes. The first teambuilding meeting was then held. The meeting was held off the plant site free of interrupting telephone calls and messengers. Each meeting typically lasted one-half to one day.

The purpose of this first meeting was to review the interview notes and to modify, add, or delete items as the group saw fit. The facilitator checked the accuracy/clarity of the notes by calling on people at random to explain the meaning of a given statement and then determining if there was consensus on the explanation.

The group examined the themes (e.g., safety, trust, job posting) and placed those that were related in the same category. The group then prioritized the categories in the order that they wished them to be addressed. Examples of three key issues selected in one initial teambuilding session were the following: job posting, truck driver training on safety, and training of supervisors to ensure consistency and uniformity in dealing with subordinates.

The group then divided into two or more subgroups. The people in the subgroups chose one of the priority items from the previous step. Each subgroup consisted of union and management personnel. The purpose of each subgroup was to generate solutions to the problem. The parties were made aware of the fact that they were to develop viable proposals for solving the problem.

The subgroups reconvened into one overall group to explain their proposals and make modifications where needed. Management and the union then agreed to implement the proposals or requested time to study them. Regardless of the alternatives selected, specific action steps with timetables were agreed on at that meeting specifying who would do what in making or implementing the decision(s). At the end of this meeting, a date was set for a subsequent meeting to review progress and to set new goals. Thus, the teambuilding approach became an on-going process rather than a discrete activity with starting and stopping points.

The danger in this approach was that management and labor would fail to recognize that this was strictly a vehicle for problem-solving, not a vehicle for people to become "buddies."

However, people who solve problems common to one another generally develop respect for one another, and this is exactly what happened. Another danger was that problems that were not solved because of management or union reluctance or inability to do so could have been perceived by employees as indicators of lack of commitment by one or both parties. If a proposal were rejected and a problem failed to disappear, a premium was placed on communication to employees as to why. The minutes of teambuilding meetings were posted for everyone to read, and the results were discussed at crew meetings. As a result this danger has not materialized.

The major benefits derived from this approach have included improved communications, faster problem solving, a significant decrease in grievances, constructive standing committee meetings, and productivity/costs that were in the black in one month when similar facilities on the West Coast were in the red.

SUMMARY

Goal setting has been found to be effective with unionized employees because it injects challenge and interest into tasks. The result can be a dramatic increase in productivity coupled with a dramatic decrease in costs.

Because goal setting typically aims at increasing productivity, unions are generally reluctant to endorse them for fear of alienating their rank-and-file. The following guidelines have proven to be effective in getting union support for a plan without making it an issue for collective bargaining: (1) working to attain the goal is voluntary; (2) there are no monetary rewards tied to the goal; (3) the supervisors must exhibit supportive behavior only; (4) failure to attain the goal must not be punished; and (5) goal setting must not result in a reduction in the workforce. When these guidelines are not followed (or when it appears that they will not be followed), union/management conflicts may arise.

Goals, however, do not always have to be set in terms of

the quantity of some output measure to be produced within a specified time period. Goal setting has proven to be especially useful in a teambuilding atmosphere where the emphasis by the company and the union is on process or behavioral measures designed to improve their working relationships. The results include shorter time periods to solve problems, a large decrease in number of grievances, and constructive standing committee meetings.

11 • *Strategic goal setting*

In contrast to individual goal setting, virtually no scientific studies have been made of strategic goal setting. Thus in this chapter we are more descriptive, or more cautiously prescriptive, than in previous chapters. We report what the experts, based on the conclusions they have drawn from their consulting experience, have to say about the subject. Definitive conclusions will have to await further, objective studies.

Strategic goals are those set for the organization as a whole or a significant segment of it. These goals (whether set explicitly or implicitly) provide the ultimate standard for setting lower level or operational (e.g., unit, individual) goals. As we noted in previous chapters, after individual goals are set, action plans are developed in order to implement the goals. Similarly, strategic goals are the basis for strategic action plans. However, the strategic planning process involves much more than just setting goals and determining the means to achieve them. It includes steps that are taken before any goals are set.

STRATEGIC GOALS AND STRATEGIC PLANNING

There are a variety of viewpoints about the best way to conduct strategic planning. Derek Abell recommends that it begin with defining the business or businesses.[1] This *rational comprehensive* approach to strategic planning proceeds as follows [2]:

1. Define the business or businesses. This step is roughly analogous to defining a job for an individual employee. It is basically a matter of identifying what the company does, e.g., "We are in the energy business"; "We are in the food business"; "We are in the computer business." Such descriptions identify the basic purpose or strategic thrust of the organization.

This initial definition serves not only as a general guide to the setting of more explicit corporate objectives, but also as a constraint.[3] It limits the types of activities that a company will engage in (barring a redefinition of the business or businesses). If the definition is inappropriate, the results can be disastrous. Baldwin Locomotives, for example, defined its business as making steam locomotives. This definition served them well until diesel and electric locomotives made steam locomotives obsolete. Baldwin's definition of their business was too narrow and they failed to change it; as a result they went out of business.[4] In contrast, some manufacturers of tin cans redefined their business as that of "packaging."[5] As a result they were able to adapt successfully to new technological developments by expanding their product line.

Definitions of the business may be more detailed than a single phrase. Abell recommends that it can be done along three dimensions: the nature of the customers; the specific customer needs that are fulfilled; and the nature of the technology employed; for example, "We sell to housewives; we sell only women's cosmetics; we sell products made by others." An organization that has multiple businesses will, of course, have multiple definitions.

2. Identify the organization's strengths and weaknesses or vulnerabilities. This should be done for each functional area or product line, e.g., financial health, marketing expertise, human resources, management skills, R & D potential, manufacturing capacity, technological capability.

3. Analyze the organization's environment. This includes an assessment of the company's competitors and their strengths and weaknesses, including their technology; the structure of the industry; the demand for the organization's products; the state of the economy; government regulation; and anticipated changes in all of the preceding.

(These last two steps are obviously related, since an organization's strengths and weaknesses always exist in relation to its environment, especially the capabilities of its competitors.)

4. Identify threats and opportunities based on the above analyses. Alternative courses of action should be considered, which may initiate a redefinition of the business. Certain products or lines of business may be discontinued or modified and others begun.

5. Set strategic goals based on all of the above information, as well as various pressures from within the organization. As noted earlier, these are the goals of the organization as a whole and are the basis for lower level goals. In a standard management by objectives system, for example, goals cascade down level by level from the strategic to the operational level, until goals have been set for every manager (and in some cases every employee). Each lower-level goal is a means to attaining the goals above it.

Since an organization is simply a collection of individuals bound by a common purpose, it is worth asking: *whose* goals are the strategic goals? Implicitly, they are the goals of every employee (if the organization is well integrated), but explicitly they are the goals of the top (strategic) managers. (We will discuss specific types of strategic goals below.)

6. Finally, once goals have been set, take further steps to insure that these goals will be achieved. As noted above, goals are set for both units and individuals, and action plans are developed to reach those goals. Structural changes and allocations of resources are made to insure the successful implementation of these plans.

A classic case of successful strategic planning occurred in the Kentucky Fried Chicken division of Heublein, Inc.[6] Shortly after Heublein purchased it from its former owner, Kentucky Fried Chicken started to lose money. An analysis of the business indicated that the food was poor, facilities were old and dirty, services was slow and surly, and prices were too high. Outsiders were already writing the business off.

The top executives of Heublein, however, were more sanguine than these outsiders, and they developed a comprehensive stategic plan. They defined their business mainly as selling fried chicken directly to the consumer. They saw their weaknesses in the areas listed above (quality, service, price, etc.). This analysis was made in comparison to what their competitors were doing. The major threat was, of course, going bankrupt; the major opportunity was to make better chicken and sell it at a better price than competitors. The basic objective was to make Kentucky Fried Chicken the strongest, fastest-growing, and most profitable part of Heublein's business.

The top management team set goals and developed strategic plans for each critical issue identified as necessary for success: quality, service, cleanliness, value, facilities, advertising, marketing, staffing, inventory control, cost control. For example, with respect to food quality they asked several questions. How can we make it better? (Answer: use the Colonel Sanders recipe.) How can we do this? (Answer: train employees.) Who will do it? (Answer: the training department.) When will they do it? (Answer: within six months.) How will we measure success? (Answer: by the use of a mystery inspector who will go to each store incognito and rate food quality, as well as cleanliness, etc.) What will be the goal for each store? (Answer: 103 points; the existing average for the stores was about 70 at the time.)

The company wasted no time in refurbishing or rebuilding stores, improving inventory control, computerizing cash registers to provide feedback on the performance of each store on a daily basis, improving advertising, improving relations with franchisees, and so forth. The result within two years was a rapidly growing and highly profitable division.

A very different approach to strategic planning was taken by Tom Czepiel, Vice President of Scott Paper. He adopted a production-control system in order to insure profitability. Variations of the system are also being used by Toyota and General

Motors. At the risk of oversimplifying, Czepiel's people had accepted the following premise: price = cost + profit. If an item cost $100 to manufacture and the company wanted a 20 percent profit, it figured the sales price this way: $100 + $20 = $120. Now, if costs go up, the company just recalculates according to the formula. For example, if the cost goes to $110: $110 + $22 (20% of $110) = $132. This is the traditional method used by most American companies, barring competitive pressure or customer price resistance.

Since Czepiel is a manufacturing vice president, he has little or no say on marketing or sales price considerations. He does, however, have a major ability to affect costs. Consequently, he decided to change the philosophy of his forty key managers. He did this by adopting the following formula: sales price − cost = profit. The new formula is only a simple algebraic transformation of the earlier one, but it represents a fundamental change in the thinking of Scott Paper. See what happens when costs go up. Originally, with the $100 cost: $120 − $100 = $20. The profit is the same as in the first formula. But when costs go up to $110, profits go down: $120 − $110 = $10. Since Scott Paper does not want lower profits nor to increase the sale price, it has to find a way to lower the cost element in the formula. Producing the item with the same or better quality but at lower cost—in other words, greater productivity—is the only way to sustain profits.

In getting this point across, Czepiel informed his forty key people that they would no longer be evaluated on their effectiveness as managers; they would be evaluated on their effectiveness as independent businessmen. Consequently, the head of each business unit called a meeting of his respective subordinates to set targets and to find ways of attaining those targets. The targets represented an agreed on goal by the group for reducing costs.

After an organization has initiated a strategic planning program, each of the major steps is not necessarily repeated in detail each year. It may only be necessary to check progress on previously set goals and to check the validity of the assumptions on which previous goals and strategies were developed. If everything is proceeding as planned, only minor changes may be needed within a given planning cycle. Toward the end of a five-year plan, however, the organization may want to start from scratch again to insure that no new developments have been overlooked. Alternatively, a year can be added onto the plan at the end of each year with revisions made in the total plan as necessary.

There are a number of possible variations on these procedures. For example, an organization could decide what rate of return it wants to achieve and then designate the business segments it wants to emphasize on that basis.

Another alternative is to do strategic planning incrementally.[7] Rather than making a firm two-year or five-year plan all at once, an organization may choose the less risky procedure of defining the business, identifying strengths and weaknesses, and pursuing limited opportunities one at a time, through a series of narrower, shorter-range decisions. Depending on the outcomes of these decisions, the original direction can be maintained or changed, and the pace slowed or accelerated.

Incremental planning seems to be characteristic of successful corporate general managers, according to a very thorough study by Professor John Kotter.[8] He found that during the first six to twelve months on the job, the managers would focus on developing agendas (goals, strategies, and plans). These agendas would be quite general and loosely connected at first, but would become more detailed and more tightly integrated as the general managers became more thoroughly acquainted with their jobs. The agendas would be periodically revised and updated in line with experience and future expectations.

It is important in strategic planning not to assume that a strategy that has succeeded in the past will necessarily be successful in the future. A case in point (noted in Chapter 8) was the manufacturer of heavy paper used for quality printing. Suddenly, postal rates rose and customers demanded a much lighter weight paper. The company did not have one, and as a result they lost 70 percent of their business within two weeks. Their business went to other companies that had done a better job of planning and were ready with a lighter paper when demand for it developed.[9]

In the case of Volkswagen, the outcome was not so disastrous. When it became clear that the Beetle would not go on selling forever, the manufacturer developed a series of successful new models.

When accompanied by poor planning, ambitious goals are worse than useless. As we stated earlier in this book, the higher the managerial level at which goals are set, the more important the role played by planning. The reason for this becomes clear as soon as one identifies the differences between strategic goals and individual job goals.

STRATEGIC VERSUS INDIVIDUAL GOALS

While an individual employee below the strategic level may or may not have more than one major goal, organizations (strategic managers) always have multiple goals.[10] Thomas McNichols argues that the three primary goals for any profit-making organization are: profitability, growth, and survival. [11] Survival is a precondition of profitability, while growth is a common means of increasing profits. Long-range profitability is the ultimate goal to which other strategic goals are a means. In any list of strategic goals, Peter Drucker would include market standing, innovation, productivity, physical and financial resources, manager performance and development, and employee performance and morale.[12] All of these are assumed to be direct or indirect contributors to long-term profitability.

Figure 6, from Steiner, shows how major strategic objectives may be linked hierarchically to the ultimate goal of profitability.

In today's climate, one might add at least one additional goal: coping with (i.e., changing, minimizing the impact of) government regulation. As in the case of defining the business, strategic goals serve both as guidelines to direct action and as constraints to limit organizational alternatives. Alternatives that are believed to hinder the organization's objectives are revised or discarded.

Figure 6 • Linking Business Objectives

LONG-RANGE OBJECTIVE	SUBOBJECTIVES	SUB-SUBOBJECTIVES SET IN THESE AREAS
Make an ROI of 15% after taxes by end of 5 years (specify for each year)	Increase sales to $10,000,000 in 5 years	Market share Advertising expenditures New market penetration Redesign of products Develop new products for market Begin new R & D in selected area
	Raise gross profits to $2,000,000 in 5 years	Reduce overhead costs by consolidating functions Sell obsolete plant and equipment Reduce advertising outlays
	Build modern facilities and operate them at capacity over next 5 years	Build new buildings Replace tools Improve production schedules Improve plan utilization rates Install better inventory control Reduce defective products
	Upgrade and maintain a skilled work force	Management training programs Management additions Management hiring schedules Skill replacements

SOURCE: Reprinted by permission of Macmillan from George A. Steiner, *Strategic Planning* (New York: Free Press, 1979). Copyright 1979 by The Free Press, a division of Macmillan Publishing Co.

Strategic goals are broader in scope than individual job goals, since, as noted earlier, the strategic goals encompass and are the basis for all of the individual or unit goals, as in any standard management by objectives program. For example, a strategic goal for a soft drink company might be, "growth in the snack food market," whereas the resulting goal for a product manager might be to "gain a 5 percent share of the New England potato chip market in one year." Or to make a more extreme distinction, a strategic goal might be to "double profits within five years," whereas an individual (or unit) goal might be to "reduce rejects by 80 percent." Achieving the profit goal would be a result of attaining all (or many) of the individual employee goals at all levels of the organization.

While strategic goals may appear, on the surface, to be very simple, they are, in actuality, much more complex than individual job goals. The complexity of strategic goals becomes apparent as soon as one attempts to identify and carry out the actions needed to achieve them. For example, a goal to achieve growth and profitability in a new area of business implies a host of subsidiary goals that could include goals for financing (to get the project started), manufacturing (to make the products), marketing (to advertise and sell the products), hiring (to get the needed expertise and production capability), training (to insure technical competence), cost control (to insure profitability), research and development (to create or improve a group of saleable products). Each of these goals, in turn, implies further, narrower goals (e.g., where to manufacture the products; how to manufacture them; what sizes to sell; how to package and distribute them; etc.). Each of the above goals would in turn require an appropriate functional strategy (e.g., sell stock to finance the venture; rent or buy space for manufacturing; advertise in certain media stressing certain themes; etc.).

Strategic goals also have a longer time span than the job goals of individual employees. The particular span of time will differ with the type of industry, but ordinarily it will range from two (in the case of highly volatile industries) to as many as thirty years (in the case of mining and energy resource companies). George Steiner claims that "the typical planning period is 5 years."[13] There are, of course, exceptions to this long-range perspective. When an organization is fighting for mere survival, strategic planning may be very short range. Just attaining enough cash flow to meet the next payroll may be the major focus of the planning process. Most organizations who reach this state, however, have probably failed to do proper long-range planning in the first place.

What are some of the implications of the fact that strategic goals are more numerous, broader in scope, more complex and entail a longer time span than individual job goals? First, strategic goals typically entail greater uncertainty (and less controllability) than individual job goals. These uncertainties touch every stage of the process: deciding what goals to set, deciding what strategies to use to attain them, trying to control the causal factors that lead to goal attainment, and so on.

Combined with greater uncertainty is greater risk. The potential losses that could result from setting inappropriate strategic goals or failing to reach them are much greater than in the case of most individual job goals. Strategic errors have wider impact, are more costly, and are less easily reversible than most individual job errors. The survival of the organization itself may be involved, and concomitantly the job security of the top executives.

Further, setting and attaining strategic goals makes greater intellectual demands on those involved than do most individual job goals. A great deal of information has to be processed and integrated. Complex inferences have to be made. Numerous causal relationships have to be identified. There is constant testing and feedback. Enormous intelligence, creativity, and decision-making ability are required to perform these tasks successfully.

Finally, the attainment of strategic goals in most cases depends more heavily on extensive cooperation among individuals and units (e.g., the coordination of possibly hundreds or thousands of employees) than is the case with individual goals.

The uncertainties, the risks, the intellectual demands, and the need for cooperation are all intensified by the fact that those who set strategic goals must consider numerous external and internal forces and coalitions when setting and implementing such goals.[14]

INFLUENCES ON STRATEGIC GOALS

A key influence on strategic goals is the action of competitors, who may come out with new products or new marketing strategies or may cut prices with relatively little warning, thus requiring a response by the organization if it is to remain competitive. In the electronics industry, for example, products often become outdated soon after they come on the market, and new aggressive competitors enter the market continuously. Similarly, the demands of customers (e.g., changing customer needs), suppliers, and lenders affect organizational strategy.

Further, the economy can take unpredictable turns and twists as a result both of past government regulation and present decisions of the President and Congress. These can affect the rate of inflation, interest rates, and consumer demand, all of which influence the feasibility of strategic goals. Government regulations affect business in numerous ways. The government routinely tells business people:

> . . .where they can build (zoning), whom and how to hire (EEOC), how much to pay (EEOC and minimum wage laws), how to design the work environment (OSHA), what hours the employees can work at a given pay rate (overtime laws), when they can be open (blue laws), what prices they can charge and how successful they can be in terms of growth (antitrust laws and price controls) . . . how to negotiate with unions (Labor Department and NLRB), what insects and fish can be destroyed in the course of doing business (ecology laws), what products they can sell and who can perform what jobs (licensing laws), what amount of profit they can keep (IRS), what they can say to stockholders (SEC) . . . and this only scratches the surface. A given firm may have to deal with government agencies at four different levels [and even multiple jurisdictions within

the same level]: municipal, county, state and federal, and
the various regulations may even contradict each other, be
changed and applied retroactively, be uninterpretable, be
totally arbitrary and cost millions of dollars to implement
and hundreds of thousands to protest.[15]

In such a regulated environment long-term planning can be a
frustrating and tedious endeavor.

In addition, the values of society at large—or at least of
vociferous, self-appointed pressure groups within it (e.g., the
"consumer protection" coalition, the ecology coalition, the "social responsibility" coalition, the antinuclear coalition, etc.)—
can place additional and unpredictable pressures on organizations. Planning in the nuclear power industry, for example, had
virtually come to a halt by the early 1980s because of the opposition of certain groups, the high costs of litigation, and the
unclear position of government regulators.

The pressures of unions and stockholders can influence
strategic goals, often in the direction of pushing for short-term
results (higher dividends, wages, etc.) at the expense of long-
term gains; however, these demands can change over time
based on the economic situation (e.g., unions may push for job
security over wage demands in times of economic crisis).

In addition to these external influences, strategic goals and
plans are also affected by internal pressures. In some cases the
personal preferences of the chief executive officer will play a
major role in strategic goal setting. In other cases, such goals
will reflect the relative power of various internal coalitions.
Goals and the plans developed to attain them always imply and
involve the allocation of resources. Since resources are finite,
those that go to one project or division cannot go to another.
Thus competition may arise among key executives jockeying
for influence. Such competition is not always harmful provided
that each manager's ultimate goal is the success of the organization as a whole. Managers are more likely to work toward such a
goal if the reward system encourages cooperation.

When an organization has multiple strategic goals, all top
executives may not agree on the priorities. And the goals themselves may sometimes appear to be in conflict with each other.

Developing strategic goals nearly always requires tradeoffs among the various goals and between the short term and the long term. For example, achieving high immediate profits can hinder long-term growth if, for instance, it is achieved by neglecting capital investment. Maximizing productivity can undermine quality. Market penetration can conflict with return on investment. Cost control targets can be achieved at the expense of employee morale. Prevention or resolution of these conflicts will depend on the quality of leadership in the organization and the relative power of the coalitions.

STRATEGIC GOALS: GENERAL OR SPECIFIC?

Clearly the setting and implementation of strategic goals is a formidable undertaking. Because of this, some experts, such as James Quinn [16], argues that, in contrast to individual job goals, strategic goals should be phrased in general terms, as is the definition of the business (e.g., "increase profitability" rather than "a 15 percent increase in net income per share").

Above all, making strategic goals general allows *flexibility* in terms of specific courses of action. A goal of "growth" could be achieved in many different ways, for example, whereas a goal of "15 percent growth," while still achievable in more than one way, might limit options to those that will show a short-term payoff and involve low risk. Lyles and Mitroff, in a study of strategic planning, found lack of flexibility to be detrimental.

> Many of the organizations in [our] sample adopted plans and goals based on a specific planning process, but did not seem to have ways of responding to deviations from these goals. Their plans were rigid, and deviations became significant problems.[17]

Similarly, strategic problems, which are one basis for strategic goal setting, are often ill-defined. The above study found that 90 percent of the corporate problems reported by one sample of top managers fell in the "ill-defined" category. Premature over-specification of such problems could arbitrarily constrain subsequent actions and thereby limit the ability of the organization to respond effectively to change.

Flexibility allows some protection for the top executives from later criticism. If a company president promises to "get 10 percent of the snack food market in one year" and gets only 5 percent, he or she may be considered a failure by stockholders and subordinates because he or she did not reach the goal, even though the actual accomplishments may have been considerable. General goals are a less visible target for opponents of the top executive to attack. Consider, for example, the following case cited by Quinn:

> The president of a large consumer products company announced to all his goal of 10 percent profit growth per year. But many in the company regarded this as "his goal"—not theirs. Despite some impressive successes, the president was hung for a failure to meet this goal in two successive years while he was trying to develop some entirely new ventures within the company. When these were slow in materializing, his vice presidents gleefully saw that his publicly announced goal was well remembered at the board level. The embarrassed board, which had earlier approved the goal, terminated the president's career.[18]

Of course, specific goals that prove to be inappropriate can simply be changed. However, this is not always practical, since an organization that is constantly changing its strategic goals may be viewed as incapable of proper planning. Top executives who have to change goals constantly may be accused of incompetence.

Frank Paine and William Naumes call the practice of keeping goals vague in order to maximize flexibility "the art of imprecision."[19] An organization always has the option, of course, of setting specific strategic goals but not publicizing them. This way they are less constrained by external coalitions than if the goals were public, and yet more motivated than if they had no specific goals.

Finally, the use of general strategic goals sometimes gives

less information about intentions to competitors than specific ones (e.g., the goal to enter the snack food market does not warn potato chip manufacturers to plan for new competition).

It should be added that keeping goals general may also help to eliminate potential union–management conflicts. Some organizations, for example, are reluctant to announce specific profit goals for fear that unions will demand large pay raises that would hurt profits.

Despite the caveats of Quinn, most textbooks urge that strategic goals be specific and challenging. This advice is probably based on the findings of studies of individual goal setting. Since there have been no controlled research studies on strategic goal setting, no firm recommendations can be made on the issue as yet.

However, it seems to us that there are situations where specificity, even for strategic goals, is advisable. Just as an individual can flounder purposelessly due to lack of a clear objective, so can an organization. A floundering organization is an organization without a clear objective (or one paralyzed by conflicting objectives); it needs firm direction, and a specific goal can provide just that even at the risk of failure.[20] Floundering can occur even when the definition of the business is clearly stated.

In his prize-winning book, *The Soul of a New Machine*, Tracy Kidder relates how Data General Corp., designer and manufacturer of mini-computers, was struggling almost aimlessly to respond to the threat posed by a new high capacity mini-computer that had been put on the market by its major competitor.[21] Finally, one of Data General's engineers, Tom West, took it upon himself to set up a team of engineers and computer scientists to make a competing machine. He did this in the face of actual opposition by some members of top management! They had belatedly assigned the task of building a competing machine to their R & D group in another state and did not want to appear to be undercutting that project. West, after some political maneuvering, set a specific goal (describing precisely the type of machine that was to be made), set an impossible deadline for his team, and, in record time, developed a new computer that was a brilliant success in the market-place. In this unusual case the innovative strategic goal and plan came from a lower level internal coalition, while the resis-tance came from top management. The resulting product may have saved the company from disaster. (The R & D group never did develop a competing machine.)

A specific strategic goal may also be desirable when radical changes are to take place in an organization. At such a time a firm's employees and managers must have a clear idea as to where they should go. Black and Decker, for example, decided to change from a manufacturer of power tools for skilled craftsmen to power tools for the public at large. This was a major change in and broadening of the definition of its busi-ness and led to rapid growth of sales. This was achieved under the guidance of a management by objectives system that in-volved setting specific corporate goals.[22] A more recent case in point is General Electric Co., where the new chairman, John F. Welch, is attempting to change the company's strategic focus from short-term profitability to increased market share.[23] To do this he is encouraging his managers to become more entre-preneurial by insisting that they develop a specific plan to im-prove their market share performance.

A third situation in which specific strategic goals are advis-able is when immediate action is needed and the precise end of the action is known. For instance, when an organization loses money in a given year, one possible response is to set a goal to cut costs by a certain amount. Or, if an organization is in serious trouble, a goal might be to raise large amounts of cash, perhaps by selling off some of the corporation's assets.

Finally, specific organizational goals become more feasible and less risky to the degree that the external environment is relatively predictable. The automotive market, for example, used to show steady, predictable growth year after year, allow-ing automobile companies to set long-range targets and engage in long-range planning. The energy crisis, high interest rates, and a deluge of higher quality Japanese imports radically changed the situation; some U.S. car makers were reduced to simply fighting for survival. Certain strategic plans became mandatory (e.g., higher quality, higher gas mileage), but specific long-term sales objectives were hard to set because the external environment had become much more uncertain than in the past.

It is worth noting that a given organization may set *both* specific goals and nonspecific goals, depending on the aspect of the business involved. In their 1981 Annual Report, for example, Du Pont set some relatively specific financial goals [24]:

> to reduce floating-rate debt, including short-term borrowings to support operations, to less than 20 percent of total company debt; the year-end percentage was 45 percent.
>
> to reduce the percentage of total debt to total capitalization [which is now 40 percent] to the low thirties over the next several years.

In contrast to the specificity of the financial goals, the goals for the Industrial and Consumer Products operations are much more general:

> Strategic thrusts initiated in recent years to further strengthen and expand this portfolio [of products] will continue in the 1980s to facilitate growth. Key elements of this strategy include: pursuing innovative technology . . . growth in the Far East and South America . . . and growth in selected segments of the coatings markets.

Here the emphasis is on improvement in performance, but no quantitative objectives are indicated. Perhaps Du Pont believes that financial objectives involve fewer unknowns and therefore are more in their control than operations objectives. Thus announcing them is less risky than in the case of objectives for operations where results can be affected by unpredictable economic and competitive forces.

Compare Du Pont with Beatrice Foods [25], whose 1981 Annual Report also lists a mixture of specific and general goals:

> Return on equity 18% [3.5% above the present level]
> Market leadership

Net earnings growth 16% [per year]
Diversification
Real growth to 5% [per year]
Community responsibility

Specific goals were evidently set for those aspects of the business that were easiest to quantify (e.g., return on equity), whereas general goals were set for aspects that were hard to measure precisely (e.g., diversification; note: the goal of diversification indicates that the company has broadened the definition of its business). In announcing actual profit and growth goals, they were taking a greater risk than Du Pont, which confined their financial goals to debt ratios. Some protection against uncertainty and risk was achieved, however, by stretching out the time span to five years and by not announcing specific goals for individual business lines or profit centers. Poor results in one area could be compensated for by good results in another; thus the strategic goals could be reached even if certain units did not reach their goals. [Note: A recent article in *Fortune*, Sept. 20, 1982, indicates that due to a number of strategic errors in acquisition, Beatrice may show a disappointing return on investment in the next few years.]

In contrast to Du Pont and Beatrice Foods, Tenneco [26] (a diversified company specializing in energy) and Hecks [27] (a retailer) did not announce any goals at all in their 1981 Annual Reports. This does not mean that neither company sets strategic goals (Tenneco, for example, is known to use goal setting extensively); but if they had such goals, neither company was willing to publicize them.

It is worth posing the question at this point of what effect the mere fact of publicizing a strategic goal has on organizational performance. Publicly stated goals might give the organization less flexibility, but they might also lead to higher motivation to achieve the goals.

While there has not been sufficient research on strategic goal setting to date to justify any firm conclusions about the best route to take, it appears that a variety of options are available to an organization with respect to goal specificity and publicity. To maintain maximum flexibility and minimize the risk of failure, all strategic goals could either be phrased in general terms or made specific but kept private. Specific and challenging goals, if we can generalize from the results for individual goal setting, may give the organization a firmer sense of direction and motivate higher performance than vague goals. Some organizations try to have the best of both worlds by setting a mixture of specific and general, and public and private strategic goals.

SUMMARY

Strategic goal setting means setting goals for the organization as a whole or a significant segment of it. It is part of the strategic planning process, a process that starts with a definition of the business or businesses and then proceeds with an analysis of the organization and its environment. Strategic goals are set in response to such analyses and to internal influences, and these goals form the ultimate basis for unit and individual goal setting. Strategic goals differ in important respects from individual job goals; the former are more numerous, broader in scope, more complex, and have a longer time span than the latter. This makes strategic goal attainment more uncertain, riskier, more intellectually demanding, and more dependent on coordination of people than individual goal attainment. Strategic goals are influenced by numerous external and internal forces and coalitions, often entail conflict, and require various tradeoffs. Protection against risk and uncertainty can sometimes be achieved by making strategic goals general rather than specific, and private rather than public. General goals allow greater flexibility which may be crucial when problems are ill-defined and when environments change rapidly. However, specific goals may benefit a directionless organization or one that needs to rapidly change its course. Some organizations prefer a mixture of specific and general, and public and private strategic goals, depending on the measurability of the outcome and their degree of control over it.

12 • *Dangers and pitfalls in goal setting (and how to avoid them)*

Even the most powerful management techniques must be applied with care if they are to benefit an organization. Goal setting has its dangers and pitfalls just like any other technique. Some of these have been mentioned in previous chapters, but a full statement of them is now in order. Specifically, in this chapter we address seven issues: excessive risk taking, increased stress, failure, goals as ceilings, ignoring nongoal areas, short-range thinking, and dishonesty and cheating.

EXCESSIVE RISK TAKING

Difficult goals have the potential to produce greater accomplishments than easy or moderate goals; but, at the same time, they have a higher probability of not being reached. Texas Instruments (TI) is a case in point:

> To be sure, by forcing middle managers to set nearly impossible goals, TI has racked up signal successes, such as its terrain-following radar system for the F-18 jet fighter, its seismographic system for oil exploration that shows underground formations in three dimensions, and its family of small microprocessors used in calculators, watches, and games, and for simple control tasks. But the pressure also can lead to overreaching, as when TI lost sales of its home computer because it tried and failed to write most of

the necessary software by itself. Lately TI has encouraged outsiders to provide software.[1]

Risk can never be eliminated from the business world. Greater risks have the potential for greater gains than smaller risks, but they also have the potential for greater losses. The point is to avoid careless or foolish risks.

To anticipate risks it is useful to make a *risk analysis*. Such an analysis should specify:

1. The possible negative consequences of a given course of action;
2. The seriousness of those consequences;
3. The likelihood of the consequences occurring; and
4. Contingency plans for avoiding, limiting, or mitigating those consequences.

The prime risk-takers in any free economy are, of course, entrepreneurs. They are often willing to risk everything they have on a venture because the payoff can be considerable; hundreds of entrepreneurs have become millionaires in recent years in the computer and electronics fields. And if they lose, it is mostly their own money. Larger, publicly-owned organizations tend to be much more cautious. The risks of error are greater and the payoffs less. But no matter how great the risks one chooses, making a risk analysis is advisable.

INCREASED STRESS

Some degree of stress, including that caused by risk taking, is the price that an individual has to pay for high performance in a competitive environment. What you can avoid, however, is *unnecessary* stress. For example, goals that are much too difficult can be lowered. Goal overload can be reduced by hiring more personnel and delegating or postponing certain tasks. Goal conflict can be reduced by insisting on compatible assignments from different sources. Ambiguity can be all but eliminated by making goals specific.

Where skill deficiencies exist, training may cure them. If there is excessive uncertainty, providing or gathering more information may reduce it. A greater sense of control may be achieved by allowing more input or authority on the part of individuals who will be affected by certain organizational decisions and by developing effective action plans.

It must be emphasized that stress can never be eliminated from jobs or from life. The complete absence of stress would imply that the values at stake are not very important. And nobody will work hard for a value that is not important. The solution is not to eliminate all stress, but to better enable people to cope with it.

FAILURE

In business, or more generally in life, there is no guarantee of success. If an individual sets a realistic (yet challenging) goal, develops a suitable action plan, and works hard to achieve it, success is far more likely than if one or more of these ingredients is missing. But success is not certain. The goal may turn out to be much harder than expected. The action plan may be unsuitable for unanticipated reasons. The time originally allocated to attain the goal may not be sufficient. And more importantly, obstacles to goal attainment, which were not known and perhaps even nonexistent at the time the goal was set, may be difficult or impossible to overcome.

As noted earlier, if goals are challenging rather than moderate or easy, failure is more likely, even though performance should increase. The problem is to maintain motivation in the face of the risk of failure in attaining the goal. Failure can lead to self-doubt and feelings of inadequacy, anger (at oneself and at those who seem responsible for blocking progress), lowered feelings of self-esteem, anxiety (about the future), and/or depression. Ultimately it may lead to turnover or to apathy among those who stay with the organization, leading to internal disorganization and dissension.

However, while the above outcomes *may* occur, such consequences are not inevitable. Much depends on the organizational context in which goal setting occurs. For example, many negative consequences can be avoided if goals are treated as guidelines, not as tools to punish those who fall short. Treat goal failure (at least initially) as a problem to be solved. Manager and subordinate need to work together to insure future success rather than blaming each other for past failures.

As an example of how *not* to use goal setting, consider the case of an executive with a history of eighteen years of successful accomplishment in a multinational corporation who was promoted to head of a division. Due to incorrect information given to him by subordinates in that division soon after his promotion, he set goals for the division that were unrealistic, and therefore he failed to meet them. He was summarily fired. He had little trouble getting another job and was very successful in his new company. But his former employer had lost a top-notch manager.

In addition to a nonpunitive attitude toward failure, give credit for partial goal attainment (see Chapter 4). Performance can still be very high even when goals are not fully attained. Finally, the individual's boss should be constructive and supportive. If a goal is not achieved, the supervisor and subordinate should sit down and discuss what went wrong and what can be done to correct it (see Chapter 7). Improved action plans should be developed for the following period. The boss may need to take steps to remove obstacles to goal accomplishment. Offer encouragement along with an expression of confidence in future goal achievement.

This does not mean that the boss should have infinite patience with laggards and incompetents. Supportiveness does not mean lack of firmness in the need to fulfill the basic job requirements; rather it means a positive, constructive, and helpful attitude. At some point it may become clear that the individual will not or cannot perform his or her assigned tasks, whereupon termination, transfer, or demotion may be called for.

GOALS AS CEILINGS

While goals are intended as floors below which performance should not fall, they can easily turn into ceilings on performance. Effort can cease when goals are reached even when much more could be accomplished. Among nonsupervisory personnel this may be a result of fear of rate-cutting or layoffs, that is, a fear that performance exceeding the goal will work against the workers' interests in the long run. Sometimes this fear is justified because outstanding performance is not rewarded or even is punished due to poorly conceived company policies.

Well-designed and well-administered incentive systems will lessen the likelihood of ceiling effects (see Chapter 9), since performance above the standard will simply mean a greater payoff through one or more forms of recognition. This will occur to the extent that people understand the relationship between rewards and performance.

Careful manpower planning will reduce the chances for layoffs so that people do not work themselves out of a job. Mitchell Fein's Improshare Plan, discussed in Chapter 9, eliminates the problem of rate-cutting through a buyback procedure. At the end of each year the company may use money saved from excess earnings during the year to buy the existing standard back from the employees, who then agree to a new, higher standard for the following year.

Among managers, goals may become ceilings if there is a fear that the following year's goals will be so high as to be unattainable. To reduce this fear, insure that the manager who greatly exceeds a given goal receives special recognition and whatever formal rewards, such as raises, are merited. Reasonable goals for the following year can be assured by allowing the person some degree of participation in the goal setting process.

NONGOAL AREAS IGNORED

The purpose of setting specific goals is to focus attention and action in certain directions, meaning that certain tasks will be performed at the expense of others. Low priority goals will get less attention than high priority goals, and aspects of the job for which no goals are set are apt to be ignored. While this is often seen as a weakness of goal setting, observe that *this is actually the purpose of goal setting.* Goal setting makes action selective. Thus, if a certain key job area is not stressed because no goal is set for it, the culprit is not goal setting as such (it is doing exactly what it is supposed to do), but the person who overlooked this crucial area. If a key aspect of the job is omitted in the goal setting procedure, the solution is to set a goal for it.

A common reason why certain aspects of the job may be neglected when goal setting is inaugurated is that quantification of these aspects of the job is difficult. However, the word "difficult" is not synonymous with "impossible." Usually it is just a matter of taking the trouble to formulate a meaningful method of measurement. For example, take the often neglected issue of employee development. How does one measure subordinate development? Basically, by specifying how many different tasks at the next higher level in the organization the individual can perform. These tasks could easily be listed along with the degree of competence on each that the person has attained. Such information could quite readily be used to set goals for subordinate development.

If some aspect of the job cannot be measured at all, it is possible that either this aspect of the job has not been clearly defined, or this aspect of the job is really not necessary. Consider, for example, the objective of "cooperating with other company personnel in the attainment of organizational objectives." What exactly does this mean? It may mean supplying them with information accurately and promptly. If so, this is clearly measurable, e.g., the individual's peers could be asked to rate this on a BOS and to give specific examples of time when the ratee was or was not helpful. Or cooperating may mean nothing more than doing the parts of the job that are already included in the assigned goals, in which case this particular item could be omitted altogether.

SHORT-RANGE THINKING

Many recent articles have criticized American business executives for excessive short-range thinking, especially at the top levels of management. Setting goals for only a one-year period, they argue, fails to take into account the fact that some goals take much longer to come to fruition, including ideas that may have a greater ultimate payoff than those that focus on the short run.

This criticism may or may not be valid, but in relation to goal setting the basic issue to hold in mind is that *the individual will stress whatever time span is applied to or contained in the goal.* Thus, if daily goals are assigned, the time focus will be one day. If six-month goals are set, actions will be directed accordingly. To stress long-range thinking, all that needs to be done is to set long-range goals. At the top levels of management, this may involve two-, three-, and five-year plans. Executive compensation may even be tied to these goals, a procedure that might reduce executive turnover. This is currently being done at General Motors. To make such long-term goals psychologically meaningful, shorter term subgoals can be set in order to indicate an appropriate rate of progress toward the long-term goals. If subgoals are chronically not being reached or even approached, it may mean that the action plan needs modification. However, some plans that do not pay off in the short run may still be sound and require a certain minimum time to pay off. Deciding when to abandon a plan and when to stick with it is, of course, a problem that falls within the realm of decision-making.

Another aspect of short-range thinking involves the temptation of some managers to take shortcuts so that the short-term results will look good. This occurs at the expense of long-term effectiveness. For example, a manager anxious to get immediate results may put heavy and unreasonable pressure on subordinates. This may work in the short run, but eventually they may get fed up and quit; this is especially damaging if they are the most competent employees. Or a plant manager may cut short-term costs by failing to perform regular maintenance on the machinery; hence breakdowns may occur more frequently the next year (when he or she is safely assigned to another location). Or a top manager may neglect capital investment to make this year's balance sheet look good, at the expense of profit in future years when the company may find itself at a serious competitive disadvantage. For example, Professor Stephen Carroll reports that:

> In the mid 1970s a large multinational company which had been using an MBO system for many years bought out a smaller company which made a product similar to one in their product line. The acquired company had been managed by its founder for many years and had a successful product which was well regarded by its users for its quality in both commercial and consumer applications. The company under its owner–founder had traditionally used what might be described as a "do your best" philosophy. It would take and accept all the business it was given, but managers did not consciously attempt to reach specific, pre-established goals. After the company was purchased, a former marketing vice president of the parent corporation (a strong believer in MBO) was made president of the acquired company. He immediately established a vigorous MBO program which was very similar to that of the parent company. He backed this new program very enthusiastically. Sales and profit goals were established for the company as a whole and for all subordinate organization units and individual managers. Significant changes were made in the company's existing sales and manufacturing programs as the means of achieving these sales and profit goals. The results were startling. In eighteen months sales increased from $50 million dollars a year to about $92 million dollars a year. A year or two later, however, the sales of the company slackened and the company's compet-

itive market position started to deteriorate. This continued for a number of years until the top management group was replaced. One of the new managers decided to conduct a quick survey of dealers handling the product to determine the causes of the company's difficulties. The first dealer he talked to told him, "This product was once the best of its type on the market; now it's a piece of junk." The cost-slashing efforts to increase sales had worked for a while, but they had destroyed the quality of the product and eventually undermined sales and profits. Other competitors had quickly jumped in to take advantage of this situation.[2]

One antidote to these types of problems is to specify very carefully the action plans or strategies to be used to reach the goals. The benefits and costs of the various plans can then be assessed.

This antidote is not always foolproof, however. The adequacy of a given action plan cannot always be determined in advance. And the potential costs of an action plan may be deliberately understated by the subordinate in his or her desire to achieve short-run success. This might be avoided by defining successful performances more broadly; for example, in addition to performance and profit goals, there should also be goals to keep turnover below a certain level and to invest a certain amount in maintenance and capital improvements.

Another possibility is to appraise the employee not only on the outcomes or actions achieved but on the quality of the particular tactics or strategies used to achieve them.

DISHONESTY AND CHEATING

Some years ago a major food products company set difficult goals for all of its members, including middle- and lower-level managers. This company's basic philosophy amounted to "Here are the goals; achieve them or you will be gone." In this high pressure and nonsupportive atmosphere, the managers found ways to succeed. Or rather they found ways to make it *appear* they were succeeding. They simply invented whatever figures were needed to make it appear that they had achieved the goals they were told to achieve. For a time everyone was happy. The middle and lower managers were getting their bosses off their backs and the higher-level managers were enjoying the delusion that company goals were being achieved. At least they were happy until several years later the auditors discovered that the figures had been fudged. The financial setback cost the company millions. The human costs cannot be calculated, but they must have been considerable.

In another case a manager, in the course of achieving his project goals, betrayed promises he had made to the unions. While he achieved his goals that year, the union leaders swore to get even. In the meantime, employee trust and morale plummeted.

Of course, there are some people who would never cheat even under enormous pressure, and there are others who will cheat even with minimal temptation. But for the vast majority of people, it depends on the circumstances. If the pressures on them seem intolerable and arbitrary, if others seem to be getting away with it, if justice seems removed or nonexistent, then many will succumb to temptation.

There are several procedures that will reduce the likelihood of systematic cheating among employees.

Honesty starts at the top. Susan, a legal secretary, discovered that her boss was charging client time that he did not actually spend on that client's work. She discovered that he did this with a number of different clients. She complained to him but to no avail. "Everybody does it," he said. She then went to one of the senior law partners. He refused to do anything about it, implying also that it was standard procedure. She realized that by condoning cheating, the senior partner was virtually guaranteeing that it would be done by all the lawyers in the office. To Susan's credit, rather than play along with this dishonesty, she quit the company.

Do not use goals as devices for punishment. The function of goals is to guide action. If they are used instead as a tool for punishment, their function is distorted at the outset, as motivation by achievement is twisted into motivation by fear, and positive outcomes are replaced by negative ones. Communication from below will become defensive in nature rather than constructive and open.

Specify action plans in advance. By specifying action plans with the subordinate in advance, possible deficiencies in the plans are often discovered at the outset. Further, this procedure may reveal deficiencies in the goals themselves. Perhaps no action plans will suffice because certain blocks make success impossible. The performance in question may not be in the individual's control. Some years ago an MBO program was introduced in a number of branches of a bank. Objectives were set for each branch manager. These objectives included goals regarding deposits. The managers were told to develop action plans, but these were never examined by either management or the MBO consultant. The MBO program had virtually no effect on branch performance. Afterwards it was discovered that there was very little managers could do to affect deposits since these were determined by such factors as the branch's location and actions of the central office. Had the action plans been scrutinized carefully in advance, the futility of setting such goals for the branch managers would have been discovered and more appropriate goals could have been substituted in their place.

Specifying action plans ahead of time is especially important to prevent the adoption of plans that, even though they lead to goal attainment, will have unwanted long-term (or even short-term) consequences.

Get frequent feedback. By keeping in constant touch with one's subordinates, one can keep track of how things are going and help them overcome difficulties. Further, keeping in touch demonstrates concern for the employee and his or her problems, provided, of course, that such feedback involves genuine two-way communication rather than ritualistic monitoring.

Be open to negative information and show willingness to act on it. If it turns out that a goal is inappropriate given certain facts that were not available earlier, or if a certain plan proves to have a fatal flaw, the manager or supervisor must show a willingness to accept the bad news and make revisions in the goals or plans accordingly. This can be especially threatening to those who assigned the goals because it may indicate an error (unavoidable or not) on their part. At least it will be threatening to those who need to see themselves as "perfect." The manager who becomes defensive when threatened in this way is telling his or her subordinate, in effect, "When I am right, I am right; and when I am wrong, I am also right—so don't bother me with facts which contradict my preconceptions." Such a manager is violating a cardinal tenet of rational decision-making: i.e., gathering all relevant information, both positive and negative. The result will be poor upward communication and poor decision-making.

Goal setting is potentially one of the most powerful motivational tools available to the practicing executive, manager, or supervisor. The evidence is overwhelming: *goal setting gets results.* But these results are not automatic. Like any tool, it is no better than the people who use it. Used properly it can improve productivity, clarify role expectations, stimulate creative problem-solving, and increase satisfaction, pride, and confidence. Used improperly it can promote labor–management conflict, feelings of failure, increased stress, dishonesty, and other negative consequences. Which result you achieve is up to you.

SUMMARY

Like all managerial devices, there are dangers and pitfalls in goal setting. If the technique is used incorrectly it will not work and may even backfire. These dangers include:

1. *Excessive risk taking.* This can be controlled by a risk analyis.
2. *Increased stress.* Unnecessary stress can be eliminated by adjusting goal difficulty, increasing staff as needed, and insuring that employees have the skills needed to attain their goals.

3. *Failure, which may undermine self-confidence.* This is remedied by treating failure as a problem to be solved rather than as a signal to punish whose who failed.
4. *Treating goals as ceilings rather than as minimums.* This can be prevented by rewarding those who exceed their goals.
5. *Ignoring nongoal areas.* This can be prevented by making sure the goals are comprehensive.
6. *Encouraging short-range thinking.* This problem can be controlled by lengthening the time span of the goals. To prevent short-cutting, the action plans to be used to attain the goals should be clearly specified.
7. *Dishonesty and cheating.* These may result from assigning difficult goals in a climate of high pressure and low supportiveness. To prevent dishonesty, top management must set an example of honesty in their own actions, avoid using goals punitively, specify action plans in advance, give frequent feedback, and be open to negative information.

Appendix:
Goal setting questionnaire

1. I understand exactly what I am supposed to do on my job.
   Almost Never 0 1 2 3 4 Almost Always
2. I have specific, clear goals to aim for on my job.
   Almost Never 0 1 2 3 4 Almost Always
3. The goals I have on this job are challenging but reasonable (neither too hard nor too easy).
   Almost Never 0 1 2 3 4 Almost Always
4. I understand how my performance is measured on this job.
   Almost Never 0 1 2 3 4 Almost Always
5. I have deadlines for accomplishing my goals on this job.
   Almost Never 0 1 2 3 4 Almost Always
6. If I have more than one goal to accomplish, I know which ones are most important and which are least important.
   Almost Never 0 1 2 3 4 Almost Always
7. My boss clearly explains to me what my goals are.
   Almost Never 0 1 2 3 4 Almost Always
8. My boss tells me the reasons for giving me the goals I have.
   Almost Never 0 1 2 3 4 Almost Always
9. My boss is supportive with respect to encouraging me to reach my goals.
   Almost Never 0 1 2 3 4 Almost Always
10. My boss lets me participate in the *setting* of my goals.
    Almost Never 0 1 2 3 4 Almost Always
11. My boss lets me have some say in deciding how I will go about *implementing* my goals.
    Almost Never 0 1 2 3 4 Almost Always
12. If I reach my goals, I know that my boss will be pleased.
    Almost Never 0 1 2 3 4 Almost Always
13. I get credit and recognition when I attain my goals.
    Almost Never 0 1 2 3 4 Almost Always
14. Trying for goals makes my job more fun than it would be without goals.
    Almost Never 0 1 2 3 4 Almost Always
15. I feel proud when I get feedback indicating that I have reached my goals.
    Almost Never 0 1 2 3 4 Almost Always
16. The other people I work with encourage me to attain my goals.
    Almost Never 0 1 2 3 4 Almost Always

17. I sometimes compete with my co-workers to see who can do the best job in reaching their goals.
Almost Never   0   1   2   3   4   Almost Always
18. If I reach my goals, I feel that this will enhance my job security.
Almost Never   0   1   2   3   4   Almost Always
19. If I reach my goals, it increases my chances for a pay raise.
Almost Never   0   1   2   3   4   Almost Always
20. If I reach my goals, it increases my chances for a promotion.
Almost Never   0   1   2   3   4   Almost Always
21. I usually feel that I have a suitable or effective action plan or plans for reaching my goals.
Almost Never   0   1   2   3   4   Almost Always
22. I get regular feedback indicating how I am performing in relation to my goals.
Almost Never   0   1   2   3   4   Almost Always
23. I feel that my job training was good enough so that I am capable of reaching my job goals.
Almost Never   0   1   2   3   4   Almost Always
24. Company policies here help rather than hurt goal attainment.
Almost Never   0   1   2   3   4   Almost Always
25. Work teams in this company work together to attain goals.
Almost Never   0   1   2   3   4   Almost Always
26. This organization provides sufficient resources (e.g., time, money, equipment, co-workers) to make goal setting work.
Almost Never   0   1   2   3   4   Almost Always
27. In performance appraisal sessions with my boss, he stresses problem-solving rather than criticism.
Almost Never   0   1   2   3   4   Almost Always
28. During performance appraisal interviews my boss:
    a. explains the purpose of the meeting to me.
       Almost Never   0   1   2   3   4   Almost Always
    b. asks me to tell him what I have done that deserves recognition.
       Almost Never   0   1   2   3   4   Almost Always
    c. asks me if there are any areas of the job on which he or she can assist me.
       Almost Never   0   1   2   3   4   Almost Always
    d. tells me what he or she thinks I have done that deserves recognition.
       Almost Never   0   1   2   3   4   Almost Always
    e. if there are problems with my performance, never brings up more than two of them at once.
       Almost Never   0   1   2   3   4   Almost Always
    f. listens openly to my explanations and concerns regarding any performance problems.
       Almost Never   0   1   2   3   4   Almost Always
    g. comes to agreement with me on steps to be taken by each of us to solve any performance problems.
       Almost Never   0   1   2   3   4   Almost Always
    h. makes sure that at the end of the interview I have a specific goal or goals in mind that I am to achieve in the future.
       Almost Never   0   1   2   3   4   Almost Always

   i. schedules a follow-up meeting so that we can discuss progress in relation to the goals.
Almost Never 0 1 2 3 4 Almost Always

29. I find working toward my goals to be very stressful.
Almost Always 0 1 2 3 4 Almost Never

30. My goals are much too difficult.
Almost Always 0 1 2 3 4 Almost Never

31. I often fail to attain my goals.
Almost Always 0 1 2 3 4 Almost Never

32. My supervisor acts nonsupportively when I fail to reach my goals.
Almost Always 0 1 2 3 4 Almost Never

33. I have too many goals on this job (I am too overloaded).
Almost Always 0 1 2 3 4 Almost Never

34. Some of my goals conflict with my personal values.
Almost Always 0 1 2 3 4 Almost Never

35. I am given incompatible or conflicting goals by different people (or even by the same person).
Almost Always 0 1 2 3 4 Almost Never

36. I have unclear goals on this job.
Almost Always 0 1 2 3 4 Almost Never

37. My job goals lead me to take excessive risks.
Almost Always 0 1 2 3 4 Almost Never

38. My job goals serve to limit rather than raise my performance.
Almost Always 0 1 2 3 4 Almost Never

39. The goals I have on this job lead me to ignore other important aspects of my job.
Almost Always 0 1 2 3 4 Almost Never

40. The goals I have on this job focus only on short-range accomplishment and ignore important long-range consequences.
Almost Always 0 1 2 3 4 Almost Never

41. The pressure to achieve goals here leads to considerable dishonesty and cheating.
Almost Always 0 1 2 3 4 Almost Never

42. The top people here do not set a very good example for the employees since they are dishonest themselves.
Almost Always 0 1 2 3 4 Almost Never

43. Goals in this organization are used more to punish you than to help you do your job well.
Almost Always 0 1 2 3 4 Almost Never

44. My boss wants me to avoid mentioning negative information or problems regarding my goals or action plans.
Almost Always 0 1 2 3 4 Almost Never

45. If my boss makes a mistake that affects my ability to attain my goals, he or she refuses to admit it or discuss it.
Almost Always 0 1 2 3 4 Almost Never

NOTE: Employees who work under a successful goal setting program will tend toward the "Almost Always" side of the scales in their answers to items 1 through 28, and toward the "Almost Never" side of the scales for items 29 through 45. The scales are keyed so that "4" is always toward the "good" end of the scale while "0" is always toward the "poor" end.

Notes

CHAPTER 1

1. Bureau of Labor Statistics, United States Department of Labor, 1979.
2. Edwin A. Locke, Dena B. Feren, Vicki M. McCaleb, Karyll N. Shaw, and Anne T. Denny, "The Relative Effectiveness of Four Methods of Motivating Employee Performance," in *Changes in Working Life,* K. Duncan, M. Gruneberg, and D. Wallis (Eds.) (Chichester, England: Wiley Ltd., 1980).
3. Edwin A. Locke, "The Ideas of Frederick W. Taylor: An Evaluation," *Academy of Management Review,* 1982, Vol. 7, 14–24.
4. Edwin A. Locke, "The Ubiquity of the Technique of Goal Setting in Theories of and Approaches to Employee Motivation," *Academy of Management Review,* 1978, Vol. 3, 594–601.
5. Edwin A. Locke, Karyll N. Shaw, Lise M. Saari, and Gary P. Latham, "Goal Setting and Task Performance: 1969–1980," *Psychological Bulletin,* 1981, Vol. 90, 125–52.
6. Frank M. White and Edwin A. Locke, "Perceived Determinants of High and Low Productivity in Three Occupational Groups: A Critical Incident Study," *Journal of Management Studies,* 1981, Vol. 18, 375–87.
7. Gary P. Latham and J. J. Baldes, "The 'Practical Significance' of Locke's Theory of Goal Setting," *Journal of Applied Psychology,* 1975, Vol. 60, 122–24.
8. Locke, Feren, McCaleb, Shaw, and Denny, in *Changes in Working Life,* op. cit.

Productivity Through Performance Appraisal (Reading, MA: Addison-Wesley, 1981).

2. Frederick W. Taylor, *The Principles of Scientific Management* (New York: Norton, 1967), originally published in 1911; Frank B. Gilbreth, *Primer of Scientific Management* (Easton, PA: Hive Publishing Co., 1973), originally published in 1914.

3. Lucien Rhodes, "The Importance of Being Arthur," *Inc.*, April, 1982, 66 ff.

4. William F. Whyte, *Money and Motivation* (New York: Harper, 1955).

5. Carleton S. Bartlem and Edwin A. Locke, "The Coch and French Study: A Critique and Reinterpretation," *Human Relations*, 1981, Vol. 34, 555–66.

6. Gary P. Latham and Sydney B. Kinne, III, "Improving Job Performance Through Training in Goal Setting," *Journal of Applied Psychology*, 1974, Vol. 59, 187–91.

7. Stephen J. Carroll and Henry L. Tosi, *Management by Objectives* (New York: Macmillan, 1973).

8. R. Henry Migliore, *MBO: Blue Collar to Top Executive* (Washington, DC: Bureau of National Affairs, 1977).

9. "At Emery Air Freight: Positive Reinforcement Boosts Performance," *Organizational Dynamics*, 1973, Vol. 1, 41–50.

10. Henry L. Tosi, John R. Rizzo, and Stephen J. Carroll, "Setting Goals in Management by Objectives," *California Management Review*, 1970, Vol. 12, 70–78.

11. Jay Galbraith, *Designing Complex Organizations* (Reading, MA: Addison-Wesley, 1973).

12. Rensis Likert and M. Scott Fisher, "MBGO: Putting Some Team Spirit into MBO," *Personnel*, 1977, Vol. 54, 40–47.

13. Bibb Latané, "The Psychology of Social Impact," *American Psychologist*, 1981, Vol. 36, 343–56.

14. Bibb Latané, Stephen G. Harkins, and Kipling Williams, "Many Hands Make Light the Work: The Causes and Consequences of Social Loafing," unpublished manuscript, 1980.

15. Gary P. Latham and Gary A. Yukl, "The Effects of Assigned and Participative Goal Setting on Performance and Job Satisfaction," *Journal of Applied Psychology*, 1976, Vol. 61, 166–71.

CHAPTER 5

1. Gary P. Latham and Sydney B. Kinne, III, "Improving Job Performance Through Training in Goal Setting," *Journal of Applied Psychology*, 1974, Vol. 59, 187–91.

2. Rensis Likert, *New Patterns of Management* (New York: McGraw-Hill, 1961); and *The Human Organization* (New York: McGraw-Hill, 1967).
3. Gary P. Latham and Lise M. Saari, "Importance of Supportive Relationships in Goal Setting," *Journal of Applied Psychology*, 1979, Vol. 64, 151–56.
4. Edwin A. Locke and David N. Schweiger, "Participation in Decision-Making: One More Look," in *Research in Organizational Behavior*, Vol. 1, B. M. Staw (Ed.) (Greenwich, CT: JAI Press, 1979).
5. Herbert H. Meyer, Emmanuel Kay, and John R. P. French, Jr., "Split Roles in Performance Appraisal," *Harvard Business Review*, 1965, Vol. 43, 123–29.
6. Gary P. Latham and Gary A. Yukl, "Assigned versus Participative Goal Setting with Educated and Uneducated Woods Workers," *Journal of Applied Psychology*, 1975, Vol. 60, 294–98; "A Review of Research on the Application of Goal Setting in Organizations," *Academy of Management Journal*, 1975, Vol. 18, 824–45; and "The Effects of Assigned and Participative Goal Setting on Performance and Job Satisfaction," *Journal of Applied Psychology*, 1976, Vol. 61, 166–71. Gary P. Latham, Terence R. Mitchell, and Dennis L. Dossett, "The Importance of Participative Goal Setting and Anticipated Rewards on Goal Difficulty and Job Performance," *Journal of Applied Psychology*, 1978, Vol. 63, 163–71. Gary P. Latham and Lise M. Saari, "The Effects of Holding Goal Difficulty Constant on Assigned and Participatively Set Goals," *Academy of Management Journal*, 1979, Vol. 22, 163–68. Dennis L. Dossett, Gary P. Latham, and Terence R. Mitchell, "The Effects of Assigned versus Participatively Set Goals, KR, and Individual Differences When Goal Difficulty Is Held Constant," *Journal of Applied Psychology*, 1979, Vol. 64, 239–46. Gary P. Latham and Lise M. Saari, "The Importance of Supportive Relationships in Goal Setting," *Journal of Applied Psychology*, 1979, Vol. 64, 151–56. Gary P. Latham and Herbert A. Marshall, "The Effects of Self Set, Participatively Set, and Assigned Goals on the Performance of Government Employees," *Personnel Psychology*, 1982, Vol. 35, 399–404. Gary P. Latham, Timothy P. Steele, and Lise M. Saari, "The Effects of Participation and Goal Difficulty on Performance," *Personnel Psychology*, 1982, Vol. 35, 677–86.
7. Locke and Schweiger, "Participation in Decision-Making: One More Look," op. cit.; and Carleton S. Bartlem and Edwin A.

Locke, "The Coch and French Study: A Critique and Reinterpretation," *Human Relations,* 1981, Vol. 34, 555–66.

8. Edwin A. Locke, "Goal Setting," in *The Encyclopedia of Management,* 3rd ed., C. Heyel (Ed.) (New York: Van Nostrand Reinhold, 1982).
9. Ward Sinclair "At Staley, Management Loves Worker Takeover," *Washington Post,* April 26, 1981.
10. A comprehensive review of training is given by Kenneth N. Wexley and Gary P. Latham, *Developing and Training Human Resources in Organizations* (Glenview, IL: Scott, Foresman, and Company, 1981).
11. John M. Ivancevich and Samuel V. Smith, "Goal Setting Interview Skills Training: Simulated and On-the-Job Analyses," *Journal of Applied Psychology,* 1981, Vol. 66, 697–705.
12. Gary P. Latham, Lise M. Saari, E. D. Pursell, and M. Campion, "The Situational Interview," *Journal of Applied Psychology,* 1980, Vol. 65, 422–27.
13. John Flanagan, "The Critical Incident Technique," *Psychological Bulletin,* 1954, Vol. 51, 327–58.
14. Susan Chase, "Life at IBM," *Wall Street Journal,* April 8, 1982.
15. Gary P. Latham and James J. Baldes, "The 'Practical Significance' of Locke's Theory of Goal Setting," *Journal of Applied Psychology,* 1975, Vol. 60, 122–24.
16. Quoted in Robert Hessen, *Steel Titan: The Life of Charles M. Schwab* (New York: Oxford, 1975), p. 32.

CHAPTER 6

1. Brian W. Scott, *Long Range Planning in American Industry* (American Management Association, 1965).
2. Alfred P. Sloan, *My Years with General Motors* (New York: Doubleday, 1963).
3. Paul R. Lawrence, Louis B. Barnes, and Jay W. Lorsch, *Organizational Behavior and Administration* (Homewood, IL: Irwin, 1976), p. 349.
4. Gary P. Latham and James J. Baldes, "The 'Practical Significance' of Locke's Theory of Goal Setting," *Journal of Applied Psychology,* 1975, Vol. 60, 122–24.

5. Russell L. Ackoff, *The Art of Problem Solving* (New York: Wiley, 1978), pp. 161–73.
6. Stephen J. Carroll and Henry L. Tosi, *Management by Objectives* (New York: Macmillan, 1973), pp. 81–82.
7. Lawrence Miller, *Behavior Management: The New Science of Managing People at Work* (New York: Wiley, 1978).
8. John M. Ivancevich and J. Timothy McMahon, "The Effects of Goal Setting, External Feedback, and Self-Generated Feedback on Outcome Variables," *Academy of Management Journal*, 1982, Vol. 25, 359–72.
9. *Wall Street Journal*, April 6, 1982.
10. J. Richard Hackman and Edward E. Lawler, "Employee Reaction to Job Characteristics," *Journal of Applied Psychology*, 1971, Vol. 55, monograph.
11. Frank J. Jasinsky, "The Use and Misuse of Efficiency Controls," *Harvard Business Review*, 1956, Vol. 34, No. 4, 105–12.
12. Bernard Bass and Charles Vaughn, *Training in Industry: The Management of Learning* (Monterey, CA: Brooks/Cole, 1966). Kenneth N. Wexley and Gary P. Latham, *Developing and Training Human Resources in Organizations* (Glenview, IL: Scott, Foresman, 1981).
13. Charles H. Kepner and Benjamin B. Tregoe, *The Rational Manager* (New York: McGraw-Hill, 1965); and *The New Rational Manager* (Princeton: Princeton Research Press, 1981).
14. Gary P. Latham and Lise M. Saari, "Application of Social Learning Theory to Training Supervisors Through Behavior Modeling," *Journal of Applied Psychology*, 1979, Vol. 64, 239–46; and Howard M. Weiss, "Subordinate Imitation of Supervisory Behavior: The Role of Modeling in Organizational Socialization," *Organizational Behavior and Human Performance*, 1977, Vol. 19, 89–105.
15. Thomas L. Rakestraw and Howard M. Weiss, "The Interaction of Social Influences and Task Experience on Goals, Performance, and Performance Satisfaction," *Organizational Behavior and Human Performance*, 1981, Vol. 27, 326–44.
16. Kenneth N. Wexley and Wayne F. Nemeroff, "Effectiveness of Positive Reinforcement and Goal Setting as Methods of Management Development," *Journal of Applied Psychology*, 1975, Vol. 60, 446–50.
17. Wayne F. Nemeroff and Joseph Cosentino, "Utilizing Feedback and Goal Setting to Increase Performance Appraisal Interviewer Skills of Managers," *Academy of Management Journal*, 1979, Vol. 22, 566–76.

18. Frank M. White and Edwin A. Locke, "Perceived Determinants of High and Low Productivity in Three Occupational Groups: A Critical Incident Study," *Journal of Management Studies*, 1981, Vol. 18, 375–87.

CHAPTER 7

1. Herbert H. Meyer, Emmanuel Kay, and John R. P. French, Jr., "Split Roles in Performance Appraisal," *Harvard Business Review*, 1965, Vol. 43, 123–29.
2. Emmanuel Kay, Herbert H. Meyer, and John R. P. French, Jr., "Effects of Threat in a Performance Appraisal Interview," *Journal of Applied Psychology*, 1965, Vol. 49, 311–17.
3. Herbert H. Meyer, "The Annual Performance Review Discussion: Making It Constructive," *Personnel Journal*, 1977, Vol. 56, 508–11.
4. John Annett, *Feedback and Human Behaviour* (Baltimore: Penguin, 1969).
5. Gary P. Latham and Kenneth N. Wexley, *Increasing Productivity through Performance Appraisal* (Reading, MA: Addison-Wesley, 1981).
6. Edward S. Stanton, "The Discharged Employee and the EEO Laws," *Personnel Journal*, 1976, Vol. 55, 128.
7. Latham and Wexley, *Increasing Productivity through Performance Appraisal*, op. cit.
8. Unpublished paper by Walter E. Meyer, Senior Vice President, Personnel, LTV Corporation, October 1981: *A Process for Evaluating Senior Management Performance Considering the Environment In Which That Performance Took Place.*
9. Latham and Wexley, *Increasing Productivity through Performance Appraisal*, op. cit.
10. Meyer, et al., "Split Roles in Performance Appraisal," op. cit.
11. Gary P. Latham, Terence R. Mitchell, and Dennis L. Dossett, "The Importance of Participative Goal Setting and Anticipated Rewards on Goal Difficulty and Job Performance," *Journal of Applied Psychology*, 1978, Vol. 63, 163–71.
12. Dennis L. Dossett, Gary P. Latham, and Terence R. Mitchell, "The Effects of Assigned versus Participatively Set Goals, KR, and Individual Differences When Goal Difficulty Is Held Constant," *Journal of Applied Psychology*, 1979, Vol. 64, 239–46.

CHAPTER 8

1. Carl R. Anderson, Don Hellriegel, and John W. Slocum, "Managerial Response to Environmentally Induced Stress," *Academy of Management Journal,* 1977, Vol. 20, 260–72.
2. Carl R. Anderson, "Locus of Control, Coping Behaviors, and Performance in a Stress Setting: A Longitudinal Study," *Journal of Applied Psychology,* 1977, Vol. 62, 446–51.
3. John P. Kotter, *The General Managers* (New York: Free Press, 1982), pp. 14–15.
4. Joel Lefkowitz, "Effect of Training on the Productivity and Tenure of Sewing Machine Operators," *Journal of Applied Psychology,* 1970, Vol. 54, 81–86.
5. Orvis Collins and David G. Moore, *The Organization Makers* (New York: Appleton-Century-Crofts, 1970).
6. Berkeley Rice, "Can Companies Kill?" *Psychology Today,* June 1981, 78ff.
7. Meyer Friedman and Ray Rosenman, *Type A Behavior and Your Heart* (New York: Knopf, 1974). There have been hundreds of articles on this topic since 1974, generally confirming Friedman and Rosenman's thesis.
8. Daniel J. Wheeler and Irving L. Janis, *A Practical Guide to Making Decisions* (New York: Free Press, 1980).
9. Tracy Kidder, *The Soul of a New Machine* (Boston: Little, Brown, 1981).
10. Charles H. Kepner and Benjamin B. Tregoe, *The New Rational Manager* (Princeton: Princeton Research Press, 1981), p. 140.
11. For a further discussion of the relationship of emotions and cognition, see Ayn Rand, *Philosophy: Who Needs It* (New York: Bobbs-Merrill, 1982), pp. 7–8 and elsewhere.
12. Arthur Kornhauser, *Mental Health of the Industrial Worker* (New York: Wiley, 1965), p. 270.
13. George L. Mallory, quoted in T. F. Hornbein (Ed.), *Everest: The West Ridge* (San Francisco: Sierra Club, 1968), p. 21.

CHAPTER 9

1. Frederick W. Taylor, *The Principles of Scientific Management* (New York: Norton, 1967), originally published in 1911.

2. Edwin A. Locke, "The Ideas of Frederick W. Taylor: An Evaluation," *Academy of Management Review,* 1982, Vol. 7, 14–24.

3. Ibid.

4. Quoted in George S. Odiorne, "MBO: A Backward Glance," *Business Horizons,* October 1978, 15.

5. See, for example, Frederick Herzberg, *Work and the Nature of Man* (Cleveland: World Publishing, 1966).

6. Edward E. Lawler, "Job Design and Employee Motivation," *Personnel Psychology,* 1969, Vol. 22, 426–35.

7. Denis D. Umstot, Cecil H. Bell, and Terence R. Mitchell, "Effects of Job Enrichment and Task Goals on Satisfaction and Productivity: Implications for Job Design," *Journal of Applied Psychology,* 1976, Vol. 61, 379–94.

8. Edwin A. Locke, "The Myths of Behavior Mod in Organizations," *Academy of Management Review,* 1977, Vol. 2, 543–53.

9. For a detailed discussion of the research on participation in decision-making and its effects, see Edwin A. Locke and David M. Schweiger, "Participation in Decision Making: One More Look," in *Research in Organizational Behavior,* Vol. 1, B. M. Staw (Ed.) (Greenwich, CT: JAI Press, 1979).

10. J. E. Bragg and I. R. Andrews, "Participative Decision Making: An Experimental Study in a Hospital," *Journal of Applied Behavioral Science,* 1973, Vol. 9, 727–35.

11. Rensis R. Likert, *The Human Organization* (New York: McGraw-Hill, 1967).

12. See Taylor's *The Principles of Scientific Management* (op. cit.) for a description of the "task and bonus" system which he made famous.

13. Gary P. Latham and Dennis L. Dossett, "Designing Incentive Plans for Unionized Employees: A Comparison of Continuous and Variable Ratio Reinforcement Schedules," *Personnel Psychology,* 1978, Vol. 31, 47–61.

14. Lise M. Saari and Gary P. Latham, "Hypotheses on Reinforcing Properties of Incentives Contingent upon Performance," Office of Naval Research, Technical Report GS-11, 1981.

15. Mitchell Fein, *Improshare: An Alternative to Traditional Managing* (Norcross, GA: Institute of Industrial Engineers, 1981).

16. Richard I. Kirkland, "Pilgrims' Profits at Nucor," *Fortune,* April 6, 1981, 43–46.

17. Edwin A. Locke, Dena B. Feren, Vicki M. McCaleb, Karyll N. Shaw, and Anne T. Denny, "The Relative Effectiveness of Four

Methods of Motivating Employee Performance," in *Changes in Working Life*, K. Duncan, M. Gruneberg, and D. Wallis (Eds.) (Chichester, England: Wiley Ltd., 1980).

18. For a detailed discussion of the issue of money as a motivator, see Edward E. Lawler, *Pay and Organizational Effectiveness* (New York: McGraw-Hill, 1971).
19. Edwin A. Locke, "The Ubiquity of the Technique of Goal Setting in Theories of and Approaches to Employee Motivation, *Academy of Management Review*, 1978, Vol. 3, 594–601.

CHAPTER 10

1. Gary P. Latham and J. James Baldes, "The 'Practical Significance' of Locke's Theory of Goal Setting," *Journal of Applied Psychology*, 1975, Vol. 60, 122–24.
2. Gary P. Latham and Lise M. Saari, "Improving Productivity Through Goal Setting with Union Workers," *Personnel Psychology*, 1982, 35, 781–87.
3. Gary P. Latham, "Creating Mutual Goals Between Management and Labor," unpublished manuscript, 1982.

CHAPTER 11

1. Derek F. Abell, *Defining the Business: The Starting Point of Strategic Planning* (Englewood Cliffs, NJ: Prentice-Hall, 1980).
2. See, for example, Henry L. Tosi and Stephen J. Carroll, *Management*, 2nd ed. (New York: Wiley, 1982).
3. Herbert A. Simon, "On the Concept of Organizational Goals," *Administrative Science Quarterly*, 1964, Vol. 9, 1–22.
4. See George A. Steiner, *Strategic Planning* (New York: Free Press, 1979), p. 156.
5. Abell, *Defining the Business*, op. cit.
6. This information was presented in an invited address given by Mr. Hicks B. Waldron, President and CEO of Heublein, Inc., at the Eastern Academy of Management, Baltimore, MD, May 14, 1982.
7. See, for example, Frank T. Paine and William Naumes, *Organiza-*

tional Strategy and Policy (Chicago: Dryden, 1982); and James B. Quinn, *Strategies for Change* (Homewood, IL: Irwin, 1980).

8. John P. Kotter, *The General Managers* (New York: Free Press, 1982).
9. Charles B. Kepner and Benjamin B. Tregoe, *The New Rational Manager* (Princeton, NJ: Princeton Research Press, 1981), p. 140.
10. Max D. Richards, *Organizational Goal Structure* (St. Paul: West, 1978).
11. Thomas J. McNichols, *Policy-Making and Executive Action* (New York: McGraw-Hill, 1977), p. 200ff.
12. Peter Drucker, *Management: Tasks, Responsibilities, and Practices* (New York: Harper & Row, 1974), p. 100.
13. Steiner, *Strategic Planning*, op. cit., p. 20.
14. See, for example, Kepner and Tregoe, *The New National Manager*, op. cit.; Paine and Naumes, *Organizational Strategy and Policy*, op. cit.; and Henry Mintzberg, "Organizational Power and Goals: A Skeletal Theory," in *Strategic Management*, D. Schendel and C. Hofer (Eds.) (Boston: Little, Brown, 1979).
15. Edwin A. Locke, "Performance Appraisal under Capitalism, Socialism and the Mixed Economy," in *Performance Measurement: Directions for the Future*, F. Landy (Ed.) (Hillsdale, NJ: L. Erlbaum, 1983).
16. See Quinn, *Strategies for Change*, op. cit.
17. Marjorie A. Lyles and Ian D. Mitroff, "Organizational Problem Formulation," *Administrative Science Quarterly*, 1980, Vol. 35, 102–19.
18. Quinn, *Strategies for Change*, p. 71.
19. See Paine and Naumes, *Organizational Strategy and Policy*, p. 31.
20. George A. Steiner, John B. Miner, and Edmund R. Gray, *Management Policy and Strategy*, 2nd ed. (New York: Macmillan, 1982).
21. Tracy Kidder, *The Soul of a New Machine* (Boston: Little, Brown, 1981).
22. Henry L. Tosi and Stephen J. Carroll, *Management*, 2nd ed. (New York: Wiley, 1982), p. 191.
23. Laura Landro, "GE's Wizards Turning from the Bottom Line to Share of the Market," *Wall Street Journal*, July 12, 1982.
24. *Du Pont Annual Report 1981*, pp. 58, 59, and 66.
25. *Beatrice Food Co. 1981 Annual Report.*
26. *Tenneco 1981 Annual Report.*
27. *Hecks Inc. Annual Report 1981.*

CHAPTER 12

1. Bro Uttal, "Texas Instruments Regroups," *Fortune,* August 9, 1982, p. 44.

2. We are greatly indebted to Dr. Stephen J. Carroll of the University of Maryland for writing and giving us permission to use this case.

• *Index*

189